P9-DGF-515

ALSO BY HUGH HEWITT

The Queen

The Happiest Life

The Brief Against Obama

A Mormon in the White House?

Blog

GOP 5.0

If It's Not Close, They Can't Cheat

In, But Not Of

Good and Faithful Servant

War Against the West

Painting the Map Red

The Embarrassed Believer

Searching for God in America

First Principles

The Fourth Way

The Conservative Playbook for a Lasting GOP Majority

Hugh Hewitt

Simon & Schuster

NEW YORK LONDON TORONTO SYDNEY NEW DELHI

Simon & Schuster
1230 Avenue of the Americas
New York, NY 10020

First Simon & Schuster hardcover edition January 2017

Interior design by Paul Dippolito

Manufactured in the United States of America

1 3 5 7 9 10 8 6 4 2

Library of Congress Cataloging-in-Publication Data has been applied for.

ISBN 978-1-5011-7244-1
ISBN 978-1-5011-7245-8 (ebook)

For Elisabeth and James, their siblings, and cousins

When, in the course of human events, it becomes necessary for one people to dissolve the political bonds which have connected them with another, and to assume among the powers of the earth, the separate and equal station to which the laws of nature and of nature's God entitle them, a decent respect to the opinions of mankind requires that they should declare the causes which impel them to the separation.

We hold these truths to be self-evident, that all men are created equal, that they are endowed by their Creator with certain unalienable rights, that among these are life, liberty and the pursuit of happiness. That to secure these rights, governments are instituted among men, deriving their just powers from the consent of the governed. That whenever any form of government becomes destructive to these ends, it is the right of the people to alter or to abolish it, and to institute new government, laying its foundation on such principles and organizing its powers in such form, as to them shall seem most likely to effect their safety and happiness. Prudence, indeed, will dictate that governments long established should not be changed for light and transient causes; and accordingly all experience hath shown that mankind are more disposed to suffer, while evils are sufferable, than to right themselves by abolishing the forms to which they are accustomed. But when a long train of abuses and usurpations, pursuing invariably the same object evinces a design to reduce them under absolute despotism, it is their right, it is their duty, to throw off such government, and to provide new guards for their future security.

—THE DECLARATION OF INDEPENDENCE

We the People of the United States, in Order to form a more perfect Union, establish Justice, insure domestic Tranquility, provide for the common defence, promote the general Welfare, and secure the Blessings of Liberty to ourselves and our Posterity, do ordain and establish this Constitution for the United States of America.

—PREAMBLE TO THE UNITED STATES CONSTITUTION

Fellow-Countrymen:

At this second appearing to take the oath of the Presidential office there is less occasion for an extended address than there was at the first. Then a statement somewhat in detail of a course to be pursued seemed fitting and proper. Now, at the expiration of four years, during which public declarations have been constantly called forth on every point and phase of the great contest which still absorbs the attention and engrosses the energies of the nation, little that is new could be presented. The progress of our arms, upon which all else chiefly depends, is as well known to the public as to myself, and it is, I trust, reasonably satisfactory and encouraging to all. With high hope for the future, no prediction in regard to it is ventured.

On the occasion corresponding to this four years ago all thoughts were anxiously directed to an impending civil war. All dreaded it, all sought to avert it. While the inaugural address was being delivered from this place, devoted altogether to saving the Union without war, insurgent agents were in the city seeking to destroy it without war—seeking to dissolve the Union and divide effects by negotiation. Both parties deprecated war, but one of them would make war rather than let the nation survive, and the other would accept war rather than let it perish, and the war came.

One-eighth of the whole population were colored slaves, not distributed generally over the Union, but localized in the southern part of it. These slaves constituted a peculiar and powerful interest. All knew that this interest was somehow the cause of the war. To strengthen, perpetuate, and extend this interest was the object for which the insurgents would rend the Union even by war, while the Government claimed no right to do more than to restrict the territorial enlargement of it. Neither party expected for the war the magnitude or the duration which it has already attained. Neither anticipated that the cause of the conflict might cease with or even before the conflict itself should cease. Each looked for an easier triumph, and a result less fundamental and astounding. Both read the same Bible and pray to the same God, and each invokes His aid against the other. It may seem strange that any men should dare to ask a just God's assistance in wringing their bread from the sweat of other men's faces, but let us judge not, that we be not judged. The prayers of both could not be answered. That of neither has been answered fully. The Almighty has His own purposes. "Woe unto the world because of offenses; for it must needs be that offenses come, but woe to that man by whom the offense cometh." If we shall suppose that American slavery is one of those offenses which, in the providence of God, must needs come, but which, having continued through His appointed time, He now wills to remove, and that He gives to both North and South this terrible war as the woe due to those by whom the offense came, shall we discern therein any departure from those divine attributes which the believers in a living God always ascribe to Him? Fondly do we hope, fervently do we pray, that this mighty scourge of war may speedily pass away. Yet, if God wills that it continue until all the wealth piled by the bondsman's two hundred and fifty years of unrequited toil shall be sunk, and until every drop of blood drawn with the lash shall be paid by another drawn with the sword, as was said three thousand years ago, so still it must be said "the judgments of the Lord are true and righteous altogether."

With malice toward none, with charity for all, with firmness in the right as God gives us to see the right, let us strive on to finish the work we are in, to bind up the nation's wounds, to care for him who shall have borne the battle and for his widow and his orphan, to do all which may achieve and cherish a just and lasting peace among ourselves and with all nations.

—ABRAHAM LINCOLN,
THE SECOND INAUGURAL ADDRESS

Contents

The Fourth Way

I

Preface

"With All Deliberate Speed"

For the first time in twelve years, there is a new "unified GOP government" in Washington—and we don't know how it will govern. What we do know is that its leaders—President Donald Trump, Vice President Mike Pence, Speaker Paul Ryan, and Senate Majority Leader Mitch McConnell—will abandon the disastrous policies of the Obama years. But they won't go back to the years of George W. Bush, when the party held fleeting majorities that vanished with a single senator's switch in party affiliation in 2001 and then again in an ill-conceived attempt by the president to use all of his political capital on Social Security reform in 2005, and Iraq's deterioration into full-scale civil war and the resulting American casualties. While W would rescue Iraq with the Surge, it was too late to save the GOP majorities in the House and the Senate. "Compassionate conservatism" died, and with it the hope for a reinvention of Reaganism in pastels. The long war made George W.

Bush's administration less a conservative government than a simple war-fighting government.

FDR invented the first modern American government, and Ike, Kennedy, Johnson, and even Nixon refined that continually growing administrative state. Reagan changed things. His "Second Way" government embraced real "rollback" of communism abroad and enacted massive tax cuts at home—although not much regulatory rollback—and it worked. Spectacularly.

Then came the "Third Way" politics of the 1990s.

I doubt very much President Trump will use the vaunted "Third Way" of politics, nor the first or second ways. Trump will invent (or more accurately rediscover) a "Fourth Way."

Former British prime minister Tony Blair is the political leader most closely associated with this "Third Way"—the politics of self-labeled centrists in the United Kingdom eager to avoid being lumped with the hard-line socialist left in Great Britain's Labour Party while also seeking to distance themselves from Margaret Thatcher's Conservative Party. Blair's "Third Way" had much in common with Bill Clinton's "New Democrats" sloganeering. Both men tried to sell the world a supposed ideological restructuring of their respective parties.

The "Third Way" gradually morphed into an ideological pose of entrenched elites on both sides of the Atlantic: small groups of self-congratulatory elected officials, experts, and their financial and media partners concentrated in key urban centers like London and New York, Brussels and Washington, D.C., Silicon Valley and Hollywood. The "Third Way" is a mind-set as much as it is a set of policies, a sense of superiority and entitlement that connects people in power via a common language of nods and nudges. The "Third Way" is very much the "Inner Ring" C. S. Lewis warned of in his Memorial Lecture by the same name he delivered at King's College in 1944. The "Third Way" depends upon start-up wealth and the fatal presumption that success at "A" means knowledge of "B" and competence at "C." Controversial Trump senior advisor Stephen Bannon refers to the "party of Davos," and whether you agree with none, some, or all of Bannon's alleged positions—I've never met him or interviewed him on the air—the ring of truth peals out from that phrase. The "party of Davos" is the party of mosquito nets for Africa instead of DDT, of Common Core from the top down instead of local control of curricula, and of a global warming regulatory regime that would deny industrialization to the masses in China and India even as it taxes the American economy into deindustrialization.

The "Third Way" was particularly bent on the idea of a world without borders, a world of transnational institutions that frowned greatly on nation-states identity. The "Third Way" consciously confused that deep belief in American or Western exceptionalism with racial or religious supremacy. The "Third Way" is deeply hostile to religion, especially traditional Christianity and its parent Judaism, and is often infused with at least a sneer of real, ugly anti-Semitism.

The "Third Way" believes itself morally superior to Reagan's "Second Way" in every way, and the insufferable arrogance dripped out of every panel discussion on almost every major cable and network television show for two decades in America, and seems to live permanently in the European press. Not even the Syrian crisis and a genocide leading to the migration of millions could shock the party of Davos into believing that the new century threatens all of the horrors of the last.

In recent years, however, the "Third Way" has been decisively defeated across the West: In Israel, with the rise of Likud's simple majority in the fractious Knesset. In Great Britain, with the Tories' surprise win and the even more shocking vote in favor of Brexit. In America, with the GOP triumph at the polls in 2014 and then of course the triumph of President Trump, who arrives with a mandate to do much. But he has not articulated much of his playbook. He has one, I think, and it was easy for voters to hear, if singularly difficult for elites to pick up on. "Media took Donald Trump literally, but not seriously," the *Washington Examiner*'s Salena Zito said in the course of the campaign. "Voters took him seriously but not literally." And voters get to decide. They voted for a "Fourth Way."

The "Fourth Way" is an old way, and it has worked before. But it hasn't really been tried since Lincoln—and before him not since Alexander Hamilton and the Federalists. Now comes the opportunity for a "Fourth Way," a recasting of long-stalemated left-right politics, absorbing most of the traditional Reagan agenda (and methods)—free markets and strong defense—while adding an emphasis on improvements in infrastructure and modernized delivery of those parts of government that cannot be replaced by the private sector.

President Trump, Vice President Pence, Speaker Ryan, and Senate Majority Leader McConnell—and the administration and Congressional caucuses they lead—have it within their power to remake America into a booming, generous, open-handed Republic of Virtue, a land of great and growing happiness in a world of great and growing happiness.

This was the Framers' vision, marred as it was by the awful—but at the time necessary compromises—over slavery, a vision improved upon by Abraham Lincoln and refined for the postwar era by Ronald Reagan. They can govern joyously, purposefully, and powerfully if their central purpose is to seek human flourishing by securing it first for Americans and then beyond America's borders. To do this, they must keep the key metric for that flourishing always in sight: the ongoing, incremental expansion of liberty and literacy around the globe in a growing number of stable regimes either of the West or allied to its goals.

That's a mouthful. But it's the key thing to get right from the start. If they start small and slow, the new unified GOP government—the first in nearly ninety years, not counting the five-month majority in the Senate in 2001 and the 109th Congress of 2005–2006—will fail.

The cliché is familiar: "If you want to go fast, go alone. If you want to go far, go together." That's an excuse for timidity, a failure of leadership. The GOP needs to lead the country very far and very fast, accomplishing much in the twenty-one months before this Congress goes home to campaign on its record. This book is about what that record could look like—and should look like.

This book is based on my twenty-seven years in broadcast journalism and a similar number in public service. My first job out of college was as a researcher for David Eisenhower on a book about his grandfather's wartime command. I then worked as a ghostwriter for Richard Nixon, spending hundreds of hours with the former president at the Elba of America, San Clemente, and then in New York, scribbling away on parts of what would become the bestseller *The Real War*, which had a huge impact on the 1980 campaign. After law school at the University of Michigan and a clerkship on the U.S. Court of Appeals for the D.C. Circuit, I became the special assistant to two attorneys general—William French Smith and Edwin Meese—preparing the surveillance applications they signed off on and doing other tasks assigned to young lawyers who stay up all night. I continued on to the post of assistant counsel in the White House, learning the various ways of that building, as well as the art of quiet, effective counseling from Fred Fielding and Dick Hauser. That led to stints as general counsel of both the National Endowment for the Humanities and the Office of Personnel Management (OPM). At OPM I was eventually promoted to deputy director of the six-thousand-person-strong agency. I became its acting director just in time for the transition from President Reagan to President George H. W. Bush—a St. Valentine's Day Massacre of a transition—before packing my bags to return to California to the private practice of law and the construction of the Nixon Library. Back in the Golden State, my public service was part-time, with tenures on California's South Coast Air Quality Management District and the California Arts Council. I spent eighteen years as a member of the Children & Families Commission of Orange County.

Most of that public service has been concurrent with private sector jobs in law, media, and teaching. I have conducted more than twenty-five thousand interviews on air and on the record—including fifteen with our new president and at least double that number with the Speaker. Those interviews, along with the time I have spent helping key leaders write books—including Richard Nixon in his exile in San Clemente, Dan Quayle when contemplating a run for president in 1999, and Mitt Romney in the run-up to his 2012 campaign—have informed the ideas in this book. I've also campaigned in person and over the airwaves for at least one hundred GOP candidates, and have known the party chairs and the activists for several decades. The book is also based on what they have taught me.

While President Trump, Vice President Pence, Speaker Ryan, and Leader McConnell (my shorthand going forward: TPRM) will lead, the GOP at every level must provide them with the political capital and cover to succeed. It is these folks on the ground who must encourage, cheer, applaud, and—when necessary—criticize the D.C. leadership. The thirty-three GOP governors—the most since 1928—and their state legislatures and state attorneys general are additional counterweights to D.C., voices that must be raised and powers that must be wielded when D.C. runs outside of the courses allotted it in the Constitution. Certainly my colleagues on the radio, whether Mark Levin, Rush Limbaugh, or Sean Hannity, or my colleagues at Salem Media, Mike Gallagher, Dennis Prager, Michael Medved, and Larry Elder, will not be quiet when we are alarmed by any actions of the new administration and Congress. Mark especially is the leading "originalist" on air and will never be shy in stating his objections. Rush and Sean are understood to be more supportive of the new president, but they too know how quickly four years pass, and while they may give him and his team more space, they will throw flags when they think them necessary. Every level of the party itself, though, must support the implementation of the Fourth Way if it is embraced, an implementation that depends on the justices and judges and their commitment to respecting the limits of government and the authority of Congress. At an even more basic level the Fourth Way also depends on the U.S. military—the finest in the world, but overtaxed when it comes to its mission and underfunded for a decade. But our ability to pay for a military rebuild—as well as for the infrastructure projects needed in the deindustrialized Midwest, and ports and airports across the country—requires a Fourth Way tax policy, Fourth Way entitlement reform, and, most pressingly, a Fourth Way rollback of the vast and growing regulatory state.

The time has come for the Fourth Way's long-delayed fight to the finish with the Third Way, the embrace of or acquiescence to the growth of a governing class separate and apart from ordinary Americans. In one of the three key pieces written during the campaign of 2016, the *Wall Street Journal*'s Peggy Noonan mused about the country splitting into a "protected" and an "unprotected" class. She was right. The *New York Times*' Ross Douthat noted that the cultural imperialism of the left had conquered and homogenized every media platform. But this left the Democrats with a "Samantha Bee problem": triumphalism and endless sneering at the rubes, which was poisoning the well in middle America. J. D. Vance wrote brilliantly in *Hillbilly Elegy* about the consequences of being unprotected and belittled in the country's small towns and rural outposts.

Those were just the emotional smacks that middle-class and blue-collar America was putting up with. Think of the crushing burden of the tens of thousands of regulators being paid to ensure that nothing gets built, combined with trade deals and labor laws that pushed jobs first to the South and then overseas, resulting in the deindustrialization of the Great Lakes and upper Midwest. The Fourth Way must address the dislocations of free trade and lift much of the absurd regulatory burden on American manufacturing and building. These new policies must then be sustained by the courts.

Selecting the right justices and judges, resupplying the military, and freeing the economy to do what this magnificent engine of free enterprise does best are the big three traditional conservative goals. But to them we must add nontraditional goals: increased spending on a very specific sort of infrastructure—done by local citizens on local needs—and on immigration overhaul. President Trump has pledged to do both.

All five goals are necessary features of one bold agenda, and this platform—which must be rapidly assembled into a coherent whole—must be pushed through into law so that voters can see and, crucially, feel the change by November 2018. The need for speed is crucial but it is also unwelcome inside the Beltway. Every day a major piece of legislation is delayed is another day lobbyists can hold fundraisers for members of the House and Senate and schedule meetings with their staffs. This is true for Democrats especially, who will have to defend twenty-five Senate seats in 2018 while the GOP defends eight. Democrats will want to squeeze every dollar of fundraising out of every day delay they can manage, so President Trump has to strike quickly and comprehensively. Early murmurings within the GOP Congressional delegation about the need for a repeal of Obamacare followed by a delay in providing a replacement rightly set off loud alarm bells, bells that will ring until repeal and replacement are accomplished. The transition back to free markets in health care can take two or three years, but the repeal law must provide a map, not the promise of one.

In defense of delay, the Constitution also hates speed, and the Framers designed separation of powers and divided the legislature into two parts, which must first agree among themselves and then with the executive before anything can be enrolled as a law. The British Parliament could and often has moved very fast indeed, but not our federal government. Rare are the times it moves into high gear. But moving at lightning speed becomes possible when the three branches agree and are not opposed by the states. Such moments, however, are rare.

The next year is one such moment—one that could even be stretched into two years with momentum and the right sequencing of initiative and delivery.

Can President Trump lead a sustained sprint toward this multifaceted package of pressing needs? Will Speaker Ryan and Leader McConnell "go big" with him? Will Vice President Pence be the bridge? Will Chief Justice John Roberts and at least four of his colleagues agree on the same sort of deference five justices gave President Obama's Affordable Care Act?

There are Article I Republicans who believe in the centrality of the legislature and the necessity of its oversight.

There are Article II Republicans who embrace Alexander Hamilton's vision of a very strong executive acting within his allocated powers, especially in defense of America's position in the world.

There are Article III Republicans who trust in the independent judiciary to curb the government's lust for more and more power over the states, Republicans who are serially disappointed in the Court's rulings.

There are even Article V Republicans who wish to take a swing at rewriting the Constitution via the convention-convening power—Mark Levin chief among them—and they will not retreat in their efforts even as they keep a collective eye on the new administration's endeavors.

And there are Tenth Amendment Republicans who believe the only agenda ought to be downsizing the federal government.

Whatever sort of Republican you are, and whatever sort of voter you may be—conservative, independent, or liberal; Republican, Democrat, Libertarian, or Green—you ought to hope for the sort of success I lay out in this book. President Trump deserves as much respect as was owed President Obama. He also deserves and will get Congress's cooperation in passing his agenda and confirming his judges.

On the last Wednesday of his presidency, President George W. Bush devoted nearly an hour and a half of a quickly fading presidency to a meeting with six conservative talk show hosts in the Oval Office. I was among them. The only purpose was a heartfelt plea by him to us that we give the new guy a chance.

I did. Obamacare was a disaster, as were the "negotiations" leading up to it. The honeymoon ended, but even then it was my way always to be personally respectful of the president on air and off because he—like President Trump now—was owed the respect that comes with the office.

Many will doubt President Trump's ability to navigate the ways of Washington, D.C., much less the world, but he has been underestimated so often as to make being wrong about him another cliché. Parties can serve the inexperienced but charismatic leader very well, marrying long experience and traditional policy positions to new energy.

"Sir, it is very easy to complain of party Government," Benjamin Disraeli lectured his colleagues in the British Parliament 170 years ago, "and there may be persons capable of forming an opinion on this subject who may entertain a deep objection to that Government, and know to what that objection leads.

"But," Disraeli continued, "there are others who shrug their shoulders, and talk in a slipshod style on this head, who, perhaps, are not exactly aware of what the objections lead to. These persons should understand, that if they object to party Government, they do, in fact, object to nothing more nor less than Parliamentary Government. A popular assembly without parties—500 isolated individuals—cannot stand five years against a Minister with an organized Government without becoming a servile Senate."

Freedom needs elected representatives organized into parties, and parties need leaders. But in free countries, leaders cannot last without the support of a party. Disraeli despised leaders who despised their parties, especially the leader of his Tory Party whom Disraeli believed had betrayed it: "He is so vain," wrote Disraeli of Sir Robert Peel, "that he wants to figure in history as the settler of all the great questions; but a Parliamentary constitution is not favorable to such ambitions; things must be done by parties, not by persons using parties as tools."

President Trump's cabinet appointments—from General Mattis at Defense to Oklahoma Attorney General Scott Pruitt at the Environmental Protection Agency—his choice of then-governor Pence as his running mate, the selection of Republican National Committee chair Reince Priebus as his chief of staff, his quick laying aside of old disputes with Speaker Ryan and former GOP nominee Mitt Romney, as well as his cordial relations with Senate Majority Leader McConnell, are all evidence that the new president understands he is not a party of one. He knows the GOP must work with him or else his presidency will fail.

Still, many worry. The left worries that President Trump is an authoritarian. The right worries he is a fraud. Almost everyone is on edge. GOP party regulars fret that the next election could deliver the sort of huge rebuke that Democrats got at the polls in 2010 and 2014. They are right to worry. President Reagan got knocked down in 1982. President Clinton got whacked in 1994. Only President George W. Bush avoided the first off-year slapdown and that was after 9/11. (Nineteen ninety was a mild rebuke of his father, with "41" losing just one Senate seat and a handful of Republican incumbents in the House.) They will all have much less to worry about if President Trump and his new team can carry the tune of governing in the "key of we."

"The Key of We"

TPRM (again, my shorthand for President Trump, Vice President Pence, Speaker Ryan, and Leader McConnell) can avoid going over the off-year election cliff. Indeed they can work a historic realignment. But only if—and there's a big "IF" coming—they govern in the key of we: inclusively, energetically, and joyously, celebrating freedom and prosperity. Americans are a happy people. They want an end to the political carnage that goes back to the impeachment of Bill Clinton, the Florida recount, the quick dissolution of 9/11 unity into post-Iraq hyperpartisan attacks on President Bush, the panic and the recriminations, the bailout and the recriminations, the coercion of Obamacare, the breaking of the filibuster, and the nastiest and longest campaign in modern times.

How ironic and very Trumpian in its unpredictability would it be if Donald Trump were to disrupt the disruption with an era of goodwill?

Democrats fear this perhaps more than anything: that President Trump leads the long-awaited realignment, a realignment delayed by Florida's too-early call by the networks for Al Gore in 2000 and then by the twin crises of Iraq and the panic of 2008. Trump owns none of that. He wasn't there. Neither were any of the other big four in TPRM, really. They were loyal to W but not, in the public's mind, front benchers. This is a new leadership team, with limitless possibilities before them.

If they get it right.

Get it wrong and the midterm elections will be catastrophic. And who knows what 2020 will bring. President Trump is certain to face a primary challenger if he abandons the GOP platform in a sustained fashion. Even a single Supreme Court nominee from outside the school of constitutional originalism would trigger a challenge, and any significant scandals will ignite an impeachment effort, which is why President Trump must insist on a "Caesar's Wife" approach to his team from day one.

Deep opposition to the structural reforms discussed herein will mean regular attempts to sabotage President Trump abroad and TPRM at home. Reflexive responses from the "Freedom Caucus" in the House or the Elizabeth Warren wing of the Democrats in the Senate could wreak havoc on the administration. So could Article I grandees sitting as committee chairs and feeling insufficiently consulted, their seniority insulted. So could out-of-control loyalists inside Trump Tower or the White House. As noted, my first years out of college were spent with Richard Nixon in exile, first in San Clemente and then during his first, tentative steps of reentry into public life. One thing a young editorial assistant glimpses from such a post is the catastrophic potential of blind loyalty. Thus part VI of this book focuses on the risk of impeachment. The discussion is intended as a guardrail, not a prophecy.

It all begins with the rhetoric of the president, the tone of his team, and the themes of his inaugural address. Many Americans are shaken. President Trump must try to both reassure and to stir—even if elites mock him, even if the cynical thump him in column inches rivaling what came down on Ronald Reagan when he walked out of the house in Reykjavik.

Longtime residents of California know what the aftermath of a major earthquake is like. Even those uninjured are jittery for weeks or even months. They're scared to be stuck under overpasses. They loathe being in Los Angeles's very tall buildings when the inevitable aftershocks roll through.

Very disconcerting—even for the untouched. Terribly hard for those who are wounded or lose loved ones.

Eventually, however, nearly everyone picks up, cleans up, shows up, and carries on. So it is with political earthquakes, too.

Ronald Reagan's 1980 victory is the closest to the earthquake that just happened; 1994 was an aftershock, even as the 2010 and 2014 elections were aftershocks of President Obama's own quakes.

"What's next?" we wonder, when the shaking seems to abate.

Many Americans worry that the Constitution is up for grabs. This is foolish. The work of collective genius that is Constitution has been tested by everything from an actual civil war that claimed 600,000 lives to various panics, two world wars, the Great Depression, and the Great Recession, not to mention impeachments and assassinations, political-judicial meltdowns like Florida in 2000, and dozens of scandals—and it does not break. It is more resilient than any other modern constitution, a remarkable, nearly perfectly balance of competing powers and separated authorities that has endured and will endure. The "civic religion" is deeply ingrained in the American psyche and all of this country's institutions. Those who fear it is off the road and in the ditch have to ignore history's many examples of America righting itself after trauma and setback. Certainly "black swans" descend and terrible things happen, but the much better bet is that a republic that has endured so much will continue to thrive under President Trump and future presidents. This is not guaranteed. It is just extremely probable.

There are enormous problems, and new ones, and of course the danger of rogue states with WMD and emerging delivery systems to hit the United States, but so too is the American military still the greatest fighting force and defensive shield the world has ever known. If TPRM move quickly and purposefully, the country can spring into a new era of "energy in the executive"—to borrow from the suddenly popular Alexander Hamilton's Federalist No. 70—balanced by a renewed Article

I power in the Congress and sustained, reasonable, and originalist overwatch from the courts, especially the Supreme Court. The balancing of authorities mostly depends on the courts' ability to check one branch's overreach against the others. With one vacancy at the top and more than one hundred below—and the "Reid Rule," which ended the filibuster on appointments—the courts can recover quickly. And to think that just a week before the election I thought the originalism movement was near death, and with it the Constitution.

This book, in its introduction and the five parts that follow, lays out the road forward. Lots of people have lots of vehicles they want to drive along the road, and that's fine. This is the big map, the playlist for the trip, the list of "must-see" stops along the way.

The preface borrows from the Supreme Court's language in the *Brown v. Board of Education* cases, which overturned the stain of *Plessy v. Ferguson* and which were the long-overdue rejection of the rotten and obviously erroneously decided "separate but equal" doctrine, a poisonous fable that so long delayed the healing of the Civil War. I wrote in 2009, on the day of his inauguration, that President Obama's taking the oath of office represented "the completion" of the promise of the Civil War amendments. And indeed in his reelection and subsequent political repudiation (despite very high personal favorability ratings), there is a great deal of hope. The first African American president was elected twice and given huge majorities that crumbled not because he was black, but because he was wrong. He was replaced by a personal opponent, one who had attacked his legitimacy in office—a wrong thing to do that President Trump has rightfully repudiated.

After a brutal campaign, President Obama and President-elect Trump sat down together two days after the election, and the graciousness on the part of both was a sight to behold. This is how we do it. This is how we must continue to do it. But the long-term continuation of the republic requires the rapid dissolution of the half-baked experiments of the Obama years and a reassertion of American leadership in the world. The great news is that President Trump has both houses of Congress allied with him, thirty-three governors eager to work with him, and a vacancy on the Supreme Court preserved for him by Leader McConnell, thus guaranteeing President Trump's immediate impact on the Court.

There is great hope for renewal, but only if all the GOP factions move forward together. By their words and their deeds, they must bring along the independents and a larger slice of Democrats than any would ever have imagined. President Trump is the leader, but all branches of the Republican Party at the federal, state, and local level must work at least most of the time toward a unified purpose.

"You cannot choose between party government and Parliamentary government," Disraeli stated conclusively and correctly. "I say, you can have no Parliamentary government if you have no party government; and, therefore, when Gentlemen denounce party government, they strike at that scheme of government which, in my opinion, has made this country great, and which I hope will keep it great."

Disraeli was speaking of Great Britain but his truth about the United Kingdom in 1848 is true about the United States in 2017. The Republican Party must be ready for the renewal outlined by President Trump in his best moments and embodied in his best appointments. If he departs from these, or if the GOP splits with him, the efforts will fail.

And thus we have to start with President Trump's promise of building things. He won on that pledge, a pledge to build new infrastructure at home and rebuild an American military, put on a starvation diet by President Obama's refusal to give it the priority it deserves. Those two promises to build have to be done the right way—and fast—if the renewal is to succeed, and the good news is that there are playbooks for both efforts, playbooks that have been used before and have worked. On domestic policy, that starts with block grants of infrastructure dollars to local boards with a national connection. With our military it begins with the Navy and Marine Corps, with large investments in the Army and Air Force as well. As fits a party that believes in local control, I begin this prescription for the GOP policy framework with the proper design of President Trump's infrastructure initiative.

II

Introduction

Governing in the "Key of We":
Jaguars in the Water, Clinics on the Ground,
an Immigration Overhaul in the Air

President Trump needs some wins, and early. Big wins. Lasting wins. Wins you can point to for decades if not centuries to come. Keeping hundreds of Carrier/United Technologies jobs in the United States was just a small, though significant, start to the wins he needs to pile up. The Fourth Way means the congressional GOP helping President Trump obtain those achievements. The Fourth Way means embracing infrastructure—but infrastructure of a different sort than is commonly thought of when Democrats throw around the term, and delivered in a much different way. It means a tenth of the federal spending President Obama squandered in the 2009 "stimulus," but a tenth yielding a hundred times the lasting benefits.

President Obama asked for and received $831 billion in the American Recovery and Reinvestment Act of

2009 (the stimulus). Asking Congress for a tenth of that amount for use in a new sort of infrastructure spending (described below) is reasonable. But this means President Trump will ask Congress for a lot of money to spend on infrastructure—big money in real terms, although small relative to the Obama stimulus. Congress should give it to him.

President Trump won on the promise of new infrastructure. And the right kind of new infrastructure projects alongside an immigration overhaul can create in one year a domestic legacy that will far outshine anything accomplished by President Obama in eight. It can be done. There is a playbook. You just have to study what's been happening in Orange County, California—specifically in Santa Ana—since 1999 and in Phoenix, Arizona, during the same period.

About 350,000 people live in Santa Ana, California. Close to 80 percent of them are Hispanic. As of 2015, there were 52,582 residents enrolled in Santa Ana Unified School District K–12 schools, so the city has a very rapidly growing population. The median age is just under thirty, with 30 percent of the population under eighteen. One in five people live below the poverty line. The residents of Santa Ana live elbow to elbow—12,000 per square mile. It is the fifty-seventh-largest city in America. Its population is often said to include the largest number of Mexican citizens living outside of Mexico, though that is the sort of assertion that cannot be "fact-checked." But we are certain that of the approximately 11 million unauthorized residents in the United States, more than half are Mexican. Tens of thousands live in Santa Ana. People with more than a casual fear of deportation are not easily counted or cared for, nor are their contributions and costs easily collected and turned into graphs, but it is safe to say that one of the physical centers of the immigration policy debate is Santa Ana.

Santa Ana is also home of a pool for the Segerstrom High School Jaguars, along with a YMCA pool next door, and Dr. Patricia Riba's "Serving Kids Hope" clinic. These three structures—technically known as "infrastructure" exist because the nine-member Children & Families Commission of Orange County (of which I have been a member since its founding in 1999) paid for most of their costs. I see in these expenditures—in the commission's organization and in its funding and spending, as well as in its results—the future of the GOP. This is a microcosm of the potential success that President Donald Trump can have when it comes to infrastructure. This is the kind of spending that juices the economy, creates immediate and sustained employment, assists the poor with health care and health more generally, and has the additional benefit of enormous political pop.

Keep in mind as you assess these examples that this is a book about (1) how Republicans need to talk about the future, how and when they communicate, (2) the rules they need to adopt to ensure that the GOP seizes the chance to become a governing majority party for a generation or more, and (3) the specific policies it needs to embrace and support—the infrastructure and immigration policies discussed herein, a 350-ship Navy, originalists judges and court expansions, as well as tax reform and a regulatory state overhaul—while recognizing (4) the tension between the Article I GOP, led by Speaker Ryan and Leader McConnell; the Article II, GOP led by President Trump; and the Article III GOP, led by Chief Justice John Roberts. Together they can open a new and wonderful era in America. If they stay apart there will be another impeachment and resignation, or a Republican primary challenge to President Trump in the winter and spring of 2020, following a massacre at the polls in November 2018. I'm counting on decision makers in each of the three parts of the GOP to be open to outside thinking. I'm counting on TPRM actually wanting to win and having the openness to ideas not of their own making.

If the GOP descends into internal strife over agendas, or goes slow in carrying out a common vision, or is undermined by scandal brought about because of hyper-loyalists to any of the principal figures, it will all crash, and in the collision of agendas could come massive political carnage which, if paralleled by any political scandal, could consume President Trump in an impeachment proceeding. At a minimum, there would be either a return to the policies of the Dean Martin Republicans, who governed the House GOP caucus from the departure of Newt Gingrich to the arrival of Paul Ryan, or the embrace of the absurd ideological extremism of the *Wall Street Journal* Republicans with their love of Hayek and their disconnect from Main Street and the ordinary blue-collar worker. Either would doom the GOP. But there is a "Fourth Way." Much like the Democrats invented a "Third Way" when their years in the political wilderness between 1980 and 1992 beat the liberal wing into submission. The Fourth Way will work—if it isn't undone by scandal fueled by an extremely hostile mainstream media, the "MSM," which is now widely understood to include not just the big networks and old papers but the new media that embodies the familiar left-leaning bias of the chattering class. Any empowerment of hyperpartisan loyalists beyond the close supervision of experienced hands who understand the risks of power could end in disaster, just as Richard Nixon's sweeping victory of 1972 was followed by his resignation in August 1974. It doesn't take long—just the blink of an eye—to fail. "He stood on pinnacles that dissolved into precipice," Dr. Henry Kissinger said of Richard Nixon at the former president's funeral. "He achieved greatly, and he suffered deeply." This is not the eulogy that Donald Trump wants. He wants a tribute to an unexpected and massively successful presidency following the most surprising election in history—the first where both parties were dumbfounded by the result. A surprise win could be followed by an enormous disaster of a presidency. Or by a stunningly successful one, every bit as unpredicted as the Trump win.

This chapter lays out the types of "infrastructure" the new president should seek to win the political future of the country while fundamentally transforming how government spending should be done, and explains why marrying these infrastructure investments to an immigration overhaul makes so much sense. Investments in infrastructure are inherently "political." The government is picking winners and losers when it invests federal dollars, which is why it is so dangerous and can quickly descend into "crony capitalism," where only friends win and enemies always lose.

Ike's interstate highway system was infrastructure, though, as were the first railroads and the Erie Canal. "Internal improvements" are made in every generation. If the right ones are made, the country benefits. As does the party superintending their construction. Make corrupt choices not based on the common good and scandal follows.

Democrats would never impeach one of their own. Republicans already have and would have removed my old boss Richard Nixon had he not resigned. Part VI of this book is a meditation on how this could all go very wrong. Parts III, IV, and V are about getting the policies right to prevent VI from ever occurring. This part is about words and visions surrounding the infrastructure and the immigration overhaul. Get this part right—learn to govern in the "key of we"—and the GOP will truly prosper, as will the country.

The vision must consist of more than speeches. We got beautiful speeches from President Obama—at least at the beginning—but they could not lift the dreadful weight of Obamacare from the economy or recover the $831 billion in stimulus that was wasted. If the GOP innovates when it comes to infrastructure investments and combines those investments with an immigration overhaul it will make the Democratic Party and its ruinous instincts of the past decade as relevant to the next thirty years as Republicans were to the thirty years that followed FDR's landslide of 1932.

And it all begins with Jaguars in the water and Christian doctors in the Phoenix barrio. It begins with Waddell Pool in Niles, Ohio, and it all depends on the GOP rejecting the extreme fringe of hate and bigotry that thinks it rode into power in November while finally doing something about the pressing need for a border fence and an immigration overhaul. This spending cares about the homeless population and acts in concert with the private sector to shelter them, not use them to score political points.

Waddell Pool was where I learned the joys of lifeguarding in the summer of 1974, fresh out of high school. My brothers made more money working at a mill, but I made the better choice, getting Red Cross certified and spending summer outside with zinc oxide on my nose, a red hat of authority on my head, and an ocean of really wonderful-looking young women around from dawn until dusk. The Waddell Pool was built in the Depression by FDR's Works Progress Administration (WPA). The WPA constructed more than 600,000 miles of roads and built or repaired more than 124,000 bridges, 125,000 public buildings, 8,000 parks, and 850 airport runways in its eight years of existence. These buildings included the structures surrounding the big pool at Waddell Park, which was still working to the benefit of the Niles community—and generating revenue—four decades later when I went to work there, and which continues to do so to this day. It is a trophy of the New Deal, one of hundreds of thousands, including artworks of all sorts, stadiums, and of course roads and bridges.

President Trump needs trophies, too. If his first bill combined a huge burst of purpose-driven infrastructure—consisting of physical structures housing real programs and endowed with the means of continuing across the country—along with an immigration overhaul (including the border fence), President Trump will have delivered. The difference between these tangible achievements with physical addresses (call them "tangible Trump trophies," or T3s) and the "shovel-ready projects" of Obama-Biden stimulus fame in 2009? The key will be that, like Waddell Pool, you will be able to point to the T3s. The T3s will have many purposes: immediate employment, lasting community impact, and health and fitness—especially for the poorest Americans.

One of the great joys of being in the radio business over the last eight years has been asking Democrats—again and again and again—to point me to any building left behind by President Obama's $831 billion stimulus. They can't because there aren't any. President Obama's stimulus was almost the reverse of the WPA. It all went poof. I like to press my lefty friends when they come on my show about what was actually done with the money. One of the brightest and most affable, Jonathan Alter, once offered up improvements on New Jersey's Route 3 as I pressed for details in September 2010. I've always loved that. Route 3 in New Jersey got new yellow stripes or something. The point is, it was most definitely not on par with the New Ramsey High School in Ramsey New Jersey, built in 1936 and 1937 through WPA funds matched by the local school district. (I know about the New Ramsey High School because my longtime pal and occasional guest host, retired lawyer and Vietnam-era carrier pilot Joseph Timothy Cook, always reminds me of his WPA-built alma mater when we talk of such things.) Maybe the 2009 stimulus helped juice the economy out of the Great Recession, and maybe it didn't and the bubble bursting worked itself out—is working itself out—as these things do.

But whatever the 2009 stimulus did or did not do, it most definitely left few if any easily identifiable marks of ever having been. Eight hundred thirty-one billion, gone without a trace. Can you imagine Donald Trump spending $831 billion and not leaving a mark? Whatever the size of his infrastructure program, you are going to see it, and see if for a hundred years.

Andrew Carnegie is another example for President Trump. I spent nearly every Tuesday night of my youth with my dad and brothers at the Carnegie Library in Warren, Ohio. I loved the place. I can close my eyes and summon its smells. I didn't realize for years that our Tuesday night ritual gave my mom some quiet time to herself, while also establishing in us Hewitt boys an insatiable love of reading. That respite and that love came from Andrew Carnegie's beneficence.

A total of 2,509 Carnegie libraries were built between 1883 and 1929, with 1,689 of them built in the United States. The libraries were built according to "the Carnegie formula," which demanded of local jurisdictions some financial contributions of their own—"earnest money" we could call it today. Carnegie insisted on local dollars mixing with his because, he wrote, "an endowed institution is liable to become the prey of a clique. The public ceases to take interest in it, or, rather, never acquires interest in it." Carnegie warned about projects where "[e]verything has been done for the community instead of its being only helped to help itself." Thus Carnegie required the local governments to:

demonstrate the need for a public library;
provide the building site;
pay to staff and maintain the library;
draw from public funds to run the library—not use only private donations;
annually provide 10 percent of the cost of the library's construction to support its operation; and,
provide free service to all.

Carnegie assistant James Bertram got the assignment of making the principles become brick and mortar. Bertram created a "Schedule of Questions" for would-be recipients, simple, direct questions that probed local need and commitment. They weren't complicated and the evaluation of each proposal was swift. Carnegie's program ultimately took nearly forty-five years to complete, but each building was an "immediate infrastructure improvement," increasing literacy while also employing carpenters and masons and staff. Tangible. Trophy. For Carnegie.

Obviously we don't need Carnegie-style libraries in the twenty-first century, though many of the buildings have been repurposed over the decades. Physical structures are capital, and though they can and do deteriorate, they last far longer and are likelier to serve more needs than do grants to individuals to seek meaning and fulfillment in self-directed endeavors. President Trump should insist on a fund of $83 billion—a tenth the size of the Obama stimulus—and it should be mixed in with lures for conservative must-haves such as tax reform and entitlement reform (discussed below).

How can President Trump use this fund to further the goal of unity in the country, even as he consolidates his political revolution? The way to do this is to create new *local* agencies, run by citizens on a voluntary basis, to which these funds would be sent and through which these funds would be spent. The job of these "Trump boards" would be to use general guidelines set by the new president and Congress to build and endow buildings and programs in needy neighborhoods of their communities. The boards' appointees would serve at the discretion of their appointing authority—the president, the Speaker, or the majority leader (see below)—and its members would be appointed by those three leaders. This highly successful model is based on the actual experience of the boards established in the aftermath of the passage of California's Proposition 10.

In 1998, actor, director, and liberal political activist Rob Reiner wanted to push for universal preschool for children under five. But he realized a mandate for such a program would be an intrusive, big-government jam-down that many parents and most conservatives would resist. So Reiner decided to slice the sausage. He began by hunting for money.

Reiner teamed up with former United States congressman Republican Michael Huffington to sponsor an initiative (eventually denominated "Proposition 10") that would add fifty cents to every pack of smokes. The revenue raised by the new tax would then be divided 80 and 20 percent, respectively, between new county commissions and a new state agency. The commissions were obliged to spend their share of cigarette tax money on programs that would work to make children ages zero to five "healthy and ready to learn" by the time they entered kindergarten.

Note the bipartisan appeal of the Reiner-Huffington project. The program was pro-life from the start, treating the not-yet-born as persons and investing in them and their moms and families. The principle of "subsidiarity" (governing from the level closest to the citizen) was also embedded within the proposal. The vast majority of the initiative's money went to new local bodies in every California county, with at least half of these commissions' appointees coming from the private sector. But the greatest innovation was that these boards had only the most general of guidelines: (1) the expenditures needed only to benefit the target audience, children zero to five *and* their families, and (2) the spending could not be simply "substitutionary" or "supplemental." That meant the commissions couldn't just throw the new dough into old county government pots. They had to spend the money on new things. All the county commissions became innovators.

I was cohost of a nightly news and public affairs show for the then PBS-affiliate KCET at the time the Prop 10 initiative went to the voters. Reiner came and stumped for it there, as well as on my radio show.

I bit. Hard. Reiner had cunningly devised a program that conservatives would love: a sin tax on smoking that would empower local boards—the majority of whose members had to be private citizens paid no more than a token stipend—to devise solutions to the most pressing problems faced by children in their own backyards. Not only did I endorse the initiative and urge its passage, but when it did pass I applied for and was appointed to the Orange County Board—now renamed the Children & Families Commission of Orange County—and have stayed on these eighteen years. This single county commission has spent $546 million in those years, directing the money to more than 260 different recipients and serving more than 1,830,000 children. Much of that money has been spent on what could be called "health and education infrastructure," with no supervision from state or federal authorities and with a staff of no more than twenty. The part-time commissioners in charge meet monthly and are "paid" one hundred dollars a meeting. It is government the way government should be done.

No public service has given me more satisfaction than this board, not even the honor of serving in President Reagan's White House Counsel's Office under Fred Fielding and Dick Hauser and alongside the future chief justice. And that is because of what the commission has been able to do for children in need in my home county through partnerships with the best and the brightest there. Along the way I've come to understand the enormous challenges faced by the immigrant community—those in the country legally and those not—the homeless community, the foster care community, and the community of families with children with autism and other diagnoses and disorders. I've also been able to hear monthly from experts about what works for these communities.

We have made the occasional expensive mistake along the way, like paying for the county to lay up antiviral supplies when bird flu threatened. But we have also figured out how to have the most powerful impact on young lives in stressed communities like Santa Ana. And we did it all at the local level, without much staff and with almost no oversight. This is how government ought to work: close to the ground, flexible, free of bureaucracy, lean, and quick to innovate. We have had three extraordinary staff leaders along the way: Michael Ruane, Christina Altmayer, and now Kim Goll. Each is a dedicated public servant. Each took guidance from political appointees and carried it out. Each was willing to push back when they thought the commissioners wrong. Their small staffs worked tirelessly. Government workers never had better representatives than the small team at this commission.

I don't intend to recap eighteen years of the commission's work, but here are some highlights that illustrate what President Trump's infrastructure investments can do.

Among my very favorite public health "infrastructure investments" by our commission is the Healthy Smiles clinic, located in the heart of the county in Garden Grove. Because of this clinic and its associated outreach programs, thousands of children are spared each year from the short- and long-term effects of tooth and gum diseases. This is basic public health for the poor. Rather than provide people with insurance for dentistry—which is very expensive and often impossible to use because of the scarce supply of dentists willing to accept minimal insurance payments—the commission funded the bulk of the start-up costs and endowment of Healthy Smiles. The idea behind Healthy Smiles is to actually provide dentistry to people who need it at a much lower cost than could a broad dental-insurance program. If President Trump followed this model and became the biggest booster of public health dentistry, with five hundred Healthy Smiles clinics opening across the United States, it would do far more good and last longer than the "stimulus" did.

Dental cavities are the single most common chronic disease among kids, five times more common than asthma and seven times more common than hay fever. About one in three kids in Orange County kindergartens had untreated tooth decay a decade ago. So kids need dentists, especially when cavities turn painful or worse and you can't sleep, much less learn.

So we helped start and fund Healthy Smiles. This year, Healthy Smiles will see 14,434 kids. In fact the number of children and family members receiving some sort of oral health service will top 45,000. Ninety-four percent of the children receiving these services are below 200 percent of the poverty level, with the majority simply below the poverty line. In other words, they'd get little or no treatment if we hadn't built and staffed a brick-and-mortar dental clinic with the help of some amazing private sector partners. Along the way the Healthy Smiles clinic has also partnered with the Children's Hospital of Orange County and the University of Southern California's School of Dentistry to train seventy-nine pediatric dentists.

Since 2001 the Children & Families Commission has spent $15.6 million on the Heathy Smiles clinic. In 2012 we transferred an additional $20 million into its permanent operating endowment. The Healthy Smiles clinic is here to stay. That's tangible, enduring infrastructure.

The cost of a Healthy Smiles program in every major

urban area in the country? Probably about $25 million for a dental clinic like Healthy Smiles. One billion dollars would thus launch forty such clinics around the country. They would never go unused if endowed. Think of all those "Trump teeth."

Tooth disease that begins with simple cavities is relatively easy to treat and even prevent. Childhood obesity is not.

The commission had a multifaceted response to Orange County's exploding childhood obesity problem, two parts of which are discussed below. The problem is real and easily measured: a consequence of the cheapest calories coming from starchy fast food and the sedentary lifestyles of children often without options—any option—for safe outdoor play and calorie-burning/fitness-inducing sports.

It is an insidious epidemic because while obvious, treatment is complex. Left unchecked the obesity epidemic will add billions of dollars of preventable health care costs to our nation. This epidemic is already well established in the adult population, with over two-thirds of Americans suffering from its long term effects. With the surge of children afflicted, it will choke our health care system in the next decade or at most two. Obese youth are more at risk for health problems once they become adults, including heart disease, type-2 diabetes, strokes, several types of cancer, and osteoarthritis. Obese children are four times more likely to have impaired school function, to be depressed, and to have anxiety issues. Childhood obesity can be stopped, however. Not by federal programs but the old-fashioned way: through activity (like sports) and good food.

In Orange County, the Prop 10 commission adopted, among other steps, two that can be replicated anywhere. First, we recruited Dr. Patricia Ronald Riba and funded her community clinic for families struggling with weight issues. Then we put the Jaguars in the water.

In 2007, the commission granted Dr. Riba $600,000 to get started as a solo practitioner in her own clinic. Because we were simultaneously bestowing a huge grant to one of the local YMCA chapters to build pools, we conditioned that grant on the Y creating space for Dr. Riba's trailers and staffs. Those trailers and the programs they house—still open because of the difficulty of finding permanent construction spending and land—have spread to many other sites and spawned numerous after-school programs. Ninety-seven percent of the patients Dr. Riba treats are below the poverty line.

Dr. Riba's approach is unique and yet basic. Her team works to address the root causes of overweight and obesity, rather than the symptoms, to ensure that the entire family becomes stronger and healthier. The intervention is the same whether the children are obese or overweight:

1. Address the psychology of feeding
2. Improve the quality of their nutrition

3. Promote physical activity
4. Assess and treat medical, dental, and psychological comorbidities
5. Empower children to grow up healthy

Eight out of ten of her patients stop gaining weight and almost as many reverse their gains at least in part. One hundred percent of her patients—100 percent!—become more physically fit. Through after-school programs stressing physical activity (running around outdoors), she and her team are developing a new generation of active kids in the poorest neighborhoods of Orange County who engage in sports and the sorts of healthy pastimes that ward off obesity.

Are there lots of Dr. Ribas around? It's hard to say, but if they exist, the federal government isn't going to find them. President Trump has to push the dollars down so that they're spent by local folks capable of finding the Dr. Ribas in their counties. Or luring them there with the promise of a funded clinic.

Dr. Riba's multidisciplinary team now reaches more than six thousand underserved families through individualized patient care plans. And Dr. Riba's plan can scale. She's very special but—and this is key—she isn't unique. What she did can be done elsewhere. Anyone looking to build a "tangible Trump trophy" just needs to replicate her program in other poor neighborhoods. The would-be T3s that find her will learn how to "do" government from the ground up, how to "do infrastructure."

Overweight kids don't stop gaining weight at age five, though, and the Prop 10 initiative said we could help children zero to five "and their families." So we stretched the rules to the limit to accomplish my own pet project: an aquatics center in Santa Ana, part of which was built on the campus of Segerstrom High School, and part of which was built on adjacent land owned by the YMCA. Segerstrom had been built with the possibility of a pool eventually being constructed on the campus, but with no money to do it. The Y had land and plans for a pool and a soccer field, but was millions short in their fund-raising because the facility would not serve the affluent or even the middle class. YMCAs have to raise money like everyone else, and Santa Ana recreation facilities is a tough ask. But they pitched me as a member of the commission, and I visited their land and saw it was adjacent to a new high school—a high school with no pool in a community beset with childhood obesity.

When my two boys were in high school more than a decade ago, they played water polo. They were blessed to be coached by an amazing man, Matt Campbell, who got them in the water early (or the gym in the off-season) and kept them there for hours. He built successful teams, and disciplined young men—and after a few years I could sort of understand the rules of the game. It didn't take long to recognize that water polo players are in fantastic shape. It is very, very rare to see an overweight polo player. Ditto swimmers. Get a kid in a swimming or polo program and they burn calories. Lots of them. And they develop cardiovascular fitness that is the envy of all athletes.

One summer league game for one of my boys was scheduled during the period when the commission was getting briefed on the local obesity epidemic at the Santa Ana High School. I got myself there, parked in a nearly 100 percent Spanish-speaking neighborhood, and walked into what is probably the worst high school pool in Orange County. The Santa Ana High School pool is old, small, crowded, and was also, at the time, the only pool in Santa Ana. The local club team wasn't very good. It was awful, in fact. There weren't many players, and the teams from down in south Orange County—mostly Anglo kids from middle- and upper-middle-class families—crushed them. There isn't a "swimming culture" in deeply Latino neighborhoods because there aren't a lot of pools. Pretty simple cause-and-effect there.

But then I noticed—and, again, it was soon after the commission's briefings on the soaring rates of adult-onset diabetes in Hispanic kids in the county—that these terrible water polo players in this terrible pool had one thing in common with their much better counterparts from down south: they were in shape. They were not obese. Bingo, I concluded. Santa Ana needs more pools. Better pools. A culture of swimming and water polo.

So, prompted by the Y's pitch and our briefings, and nudged along by my enthusiasm and the wily ways of our chair (then supervisor Bill Campbell), we found the millions necessary to build an aquatics center on land belonging to both the high school and the Y. Two pools, one center, one joint operating agreement.

"You don't have to know how to swim; we will teach you." The words crackled through the intercom at Segerstrom High School in Santa Ana one sunny morning in 2010. The brand-new $22 million aquatics center had just been finished in partnership with the YMCA next door, brought to fruition by an $8 million grant from the commission. The school's then athletic director, Frank Alvarado, was excitedly trying to drum up interest for the school's newly announced water polo and swim teams. He told the *Los Angeles Times* that for years he didn't think the school could afford a swim team, let alone a pool, but now he was proud to boast that an aquatics program was on the way. Frank was a dynamo. When I first floated the idea of a joint effort between the Y and his Jaguars athletic department, the pool was done and built in his mind in ten minutes. He truly gets the credit for making it happen—once the door cracked open even a bit, Frank Alvarado wasn't going to let it close.

Top-of-the-line pools are nothing new in sun-soaked Southern California, known for powerhouse competitive swim teams and as the birthplace of numerous U.S.

Olympic athletes. But for the Segerstrom Jaguars of Santa Ana, being located smack in the middle of Orange County didn't automatically make them part of Southern California's rich aquatic dreamland. The school was built with an empty space where a pool might go some years down the road, but so too was Woodbridge High School in wealthy Irvine. Woodbridge opened in 1980 but even its pool wasn't built until 2010. That was a wealthy district's idea of priorities when it came to pool construction. Imagine how far down the list "pool construction" is on a strapped school district's list of spending needs.

Indeed, much of the population of Sana Ana has simply never had the opportunity to learn how to swim, which creates a major drowning hazard when families head to local beaches. Jon Voget, the executive director of Santa Ana's YMCA branch at the time, told the *Los Angeles Times,* "Here you have a city with over 140,000 young people, and many kids are just not learning how to swim. They go to the beach and they just don't have the training to be safe." Voget was an early backer of the plan championed by Frank Alvarado. They made quite a pair.

In response to this drowning hazard, and with the hope that a new aquatics center could be used to promote youth development, healthy living, and social responsibility, Segerstrom High School and the Santa Ana

School District formally partnered with the YMCA—$8 million expedites a lot of paperwork—and set out to build a $22 million aquatics center, funded mostly by private donations and the $8 million from the Children & Families Commission of Orange County. Rob Reiner has no idea, but this pool was built thanks to him.

The Santa Ana School District hoped the pool could become sustainable, in part because while pools are expensive to build, swimming sports cost almost nothing to participate in. All you need are Speedos, lane lines, balls, goals, and chlorine.

"If you build it, they will come," said Segerstrom's athletic director, Nick Canzone, when asked recently if he had advice for schools thinking about investing in aquatics centers. But few could have predicted in 2008 just how fast the city's new pool would catch on and the kind of positive impact it would have on both the school and the community.

Since the aquatics center was completed, the Segerstrom Jaguars have been swimming to success. There have been two dozen "seasons" between the four sports—boys and girls polo and swimming teams—culminating in ten league championships and three California Interscholastic Federation championships. That's astonishing. That's a trophy.

"We have averaged about seventy kids per year in our Aquatics Program," Canzone proudly concluded. That's seventy fit kids ready to move on to college and the many NCAA swimming programs across the nation.

Another benefit of the new aquatics center is that it allowed the school to proudly host the U.S. Olympic water polo team, smack in the center of the poorest community in the richest county in Southern California.

Segerstrom's aquatics center has made worries like a student population that doesn't know how to swim seem like problems from a distant past. The school now looks ahead at building a list of new student opportunities like surfing and training in water safety, which is itself a pipeline to jobs and college application success.

So how about a hundred new aquatics centers at urban high schools across the country? There are thirty-seven thousand public and private high schools in America. Reliable numbers are hard to come by but it appears that fewer than a third have pools. (Of course most of those are in warmer climates, though the benefits of an aquatics center don't depend on it being indoors or outdoors.). If President Trump's infrastructure boards build pools, the kids will come and the kids will swim. And they will be fit.

Smiles and pools. And Dr. Riba's clinic. And beds. Our commission has built lots of bedrooms and stocked them with beds and all the other necessities homeless families need.

When the commission was established in 1998 there were few places where a homeless family could seek shelter as a family (fewer than one hundred shelter beds, in fact). The lack of services for families meant a well-documented local need. The building community, already organized through a not-for-profit called Home Aid, asked the commission to help support their efforts to build facilities that families could use as they got back on their feet, while staying together. Thus was born the Commission-HomeAid Partnership.

Since its inception, a dozen projects have been built. The result: 457 new transitional and emergency shelter beds across the county. The majority of these projects are small, embedded in eight different but typical American neighborhoods in cities like San Clemente, Fullerton, and Los Alamitos. The projects blend into their communities, providing opportunities for families to integrate more permanently into stable settings that allow the children to enroll in schools and their parents to receive workforce training, with a goal of gaining self-sufficiency.

There are real solutions—tested and proven to work—to meet the urgent needs of families in crisis with small children caught up in that crisis. That funding has been matched with $13.7 million in in-kind donations. The commission also works in partnership with the shelter and HomeAid Orange County to generate all possible leveraging opportunities. Once the building has been acquired or rehabilitated, ongoing operation is sustained by individual local government agencies or not-for-profits. Again, brick-and-mortar spending is key. It supplies the infrastructure around which communities of good-hearted people can organize.

Smiles and pools. And Dr. Riba's clinic. And beds.

I want to propose a fourth and fifth clinic as examples for President Trump as plans his infrastructure initiatives.

Some of life's hardest challenges have nothing to do with poverty and illiteracy but instead with challenges to the brain and body. This rising tide of "spectrum disorders" cuts across class, race, and ethnic distinctions.

Among the most common cultural identifiers of "special needs" are the diagnoses of autism and other "spectrum disorders," including Asperger's syndrome. Because of the great writing by Ron Fournier in *Love That Boy* and Emily Colson in *Dancing with Max,* more and more Americans are aware that tens of millions of American children have unique brain wiring that makes life more challenging for them and their families. Challenges can be met and in the meeting of them life can even be joy-filled beyond belief—the story of every family I personally know, for example, into which a child is born with Down syndrome.

My Prop 10 commission set out to help out county's

community of families with children diagnosed with these conditions early in our existence, beginning in 2001. We began by funding a small clinic at a Children's Hospital of Orange County (CHOC) that worked with the University of California, Irvine (UCI) Medical School to diagnosis and treat autism and related conditions.

As a small start-up this "Center for Autism" was located in just under 9,000 square feet of space, and saw 1,700 children in 4,209 visits. (We measure everything at the commission. It's the only way to separate promise from actual performance.) The annual budget of $2 million supported three staff. We learned as they learned.

Then in 2012, in partnership with the Thompson Family Foundation for Autism and in continuing partnership with CHOC and UCI and also Chapman University, we opened the Center for Autism and Neurological Disorders in its own building of 23,185 square feet, with an annual budget of $6.4 million, more than fifty staff, and a patient roll of 2,500 children who have made more than 10,000 visits to the Center in the past five years. That's called scaling what works.

The need in Orange County, as it is everywhere, is huge. Thus we have seen a 138 percent increase in visits to the center, where treatment and therapeutic disciplines and services now include these categories of specialization: Social Work, Speech and Language, Occupational Therapy, Physical Therapy, Applied Behavioral Analysis, Behavioral Therapy, Educational Consultants, Gastroenterology, Nursing, Psychiatry, Psychology, Pediatrics, and Neurology. The number of subspecialties required to assist the child and his or her family are vast, as are the number of challenges associated with these conditions.

Outreach to the community is a key to the Center's explosive growth and instant success as a magnet for families with needs. The Center has pushed a 358 percent increase in the number of parent-education workshops offering services, including an "Autism Education" series and "Families and Schools Together" programs (which help families navigating the IEP—Individual Education Program—process in school districts). The center has provided hundreds of caregiver workshops on such crucial yet basic issues as coping with tantrums, toilet training, and estate planning.

The point is that in addition to the medical needs of the patients, the center's establishment and funding provides for community-based programs that offer enrichment services for autistic children and their families, including music instruction and performance, art, dance, yoga, robotics, camps in winter and summer, and of course family and sibling support groups. Spectrum disorders impact the entire family and the center is working to expand and refine its model and in doing so has connected a community that exists, inchoate, in every county in the country.

Along the way the Center for Autism and Neurological Disorders has trained 2,400 physicians on diagnosing developmental and behavioral issues.

The cost? An almost unbelievably low $14 million start-up, funded half by the commission and half by the amazing Thompson Family Foundation. While the country was educating itself on the growing needs of children located somewhere on "the spectrum," a local commission and a private foundation leapfrogged all the studies and researchers and provided a replicable platform. Add money and grow.

Of course it isn't easy to find other doctors as amazing as pediatric neurologist Dr. Joseph Donnelly, whom the commission helped recruit to the county a dozen years ago and who, like Dr. Riba, is a hero to thousands of patients and their families. But while extraordinary, these doctors are not unique. They can step forward everywhere to provide specialized life-changing care *if* the money gets to them and houses and empowers them, not bureaucracies. I think President Trump will get this key point: it doesn't take a government bureaucracy to get infrastructure built and working. It takes trust in good-hearted citizens and a lot of private sector expertise. It isn't easy to find high-net-worth individuals to donate as generously as has the Thompson Family Foundation, but they do exist and can be drawn to follow the leads of Bill and Nancy Thompson because the "return on investment" is so immediate, the lack of red tape so obvious, the professionalism and the virtue of the doctors and staff serving this community so palpable. The generosity of already-inclined philanthropists can be jump-started with funding from Washington that is locally controlled and serves the needs of the community at their doorsteps.

This is "subsidiarity" at work, a core component of long-standing Roman Catholic social teaching and widely adopted outside of the church by conservatives of other faiths or no faith at all. The idea is that pressing problems ought to be handled by the smallest, lowest, or least centralized competent authority. Political decisions should be taken at a local level if possible, rather than by a central authority. All of our commission's work is done by a part-time board receiving token stipends (to make us subject to ethics laws) and with a very small but highly competent staff using flexibility as a tool and drawing on the best experts for the season in which they are needed. Thus three times over eighteen years the commission has retained the Bridgespan Group, the not-for-profit-sector's equivalent to Bain & Company or McKinsey & Company, to come in and audit our work and critique our grants while providing strategic guidance for the future. Humility about abilities is crucial to the success of every infrastructure investment. "We approached our work," our second executive director Christina Altmayer wrote me, "with tremendous humility. We recognized that we weren't experts in autism, pediatric care, or homelessness, but we knew how to create the environment to get the experts' best ideas and deploy them.

"As a public agency," she added, "underpinning all of this was a strong system of audits and financial accountability." She is absolutely correct about both the need for humility and the indispensability of transparency every step of the way. If you can't follow the money, the endeavor has gone off the rails, and likely into a deep ditch.

To show subsidiarity doesn't just work in Orange County, let me show you the Neighborhood Christian Clinic (NCC) in Phoenix, Arizona, and where I've been honored to speak a couple of times over the years. Unlike the programs outlined above, the NCC is funded by private citizens, not by a cigarette tax. It shows how very far public money can go if it is invested in similar models.

"The specialists could not help me because I didn't have health insurance," Alejandro Garnica, a local Phoenix resident, explained, "So my aunt told me to come over here [to the Neighborhood Christian Clinic] and finally I said okay." Alejandro's story isn't unique. Hundreds of thousands of people in Maricopa County, Arizona, have been turned away or refused medical care because of a lack of insurance or an inability to pay copays. It is these underserved men, women, and children whom the small Neighborhood Christian Clinic was founded to serve.

More than 417,000 residents in Maricopa County

currently don't have health insurance. Phoenix, the biggest city in Maricopa County, holds the vast majority of those uninsured individuals. Couple those already dreary numbers from the recent report by U.S. Department of Health and Human Services that Obamacare premiums for the "second-lowest rate silver plan" are soon to rise 116 percent in Arizona, from $196 to $422, and you have a lot of individuals who simply can't afford to see a doctor no matter how bad their ailment.

A recent report by consumer market research giant GfK found that half of Obamacare enrollees already skip doctor visits, either to save money or because they simply don't have enough money to pay their copay. Of course the health care gap long preceded the arrival of Obamacare. It has existed for decades and decades. But some don't wait for the government to fix things.

Seeing the massive need in Phoenix years ago, Dr. Paul Lorentsen decided to start the Neighborhood Christian Clinic in the city in 1999. Dr. Lorentsen founded the clinic with two major objectives. First he hoped "[t]o provide medical and dental healthcare services to the uninsured, under-served community." And, second, he wanted, "[t]o share the Gospel and love of Jesus Christ with interested patients and colleagues."

Dr. Lorentsen's dream, however, would have to overcome many hurdles before becoming a reality. A top-of-the-line dental and medical clinic that could provide affordable services to those without health care would cost considerable money. And even if Lorentsen could find enough to launch the clinic he would also need to find skilled doctors willing to donate their time to serve the clinic's patients.

Caring doctors responded to Lorentsen's plea. "There's a tremendous amount of need in this part of the community," said Dr. Philip Cooke, a dentist who decided to volunteer his time to the NCC. Dorn Dunlap, a donor and clinic champion, explained why she believed so many Christian doctors and community members decided to volunteer and donate: "Christ said the poor will always been among us, but his heart's desire is that we would not neglect them."

Early on, Dr. Lorentsen and his team decided that the Neighborhood Christian Clinic wasn't going to be completely free, because they believed that unless patients paid something they wouldn't value the care they received. Gary Plooster, the current executive director of the clinic explained: "We made a decision to have a patient charge . . . for two reasons. One is that it dignifies the patient, gives them a sense of integrity, but it also invests them into their own health care. If they're paying for it they feel a little bit more committed to following through on anything that the doctors instruct them to do."

Currently the clinic charges uninsured patients only $30 per medical visit and $40 per dental visit, relatively little compared to the actual cost of each patient's visit.

Each visit over the past five years has cost the clinic on average $128.13.

What the Neighborhood Christian Clinic can handle is impressive—from gynecology to chiropractic care—but the list of specialists the clinic can refer patients to at little or no cost is even more impressive. More than fifty are on the list, and they charge either nothing or a minimum copay. On the two occasions I have visited, Dr. David Tellez, the chairman of the board, has truly glowed with satisfaction over what he and the entire team does out of their shared mission. Of course, such a place is unique, but the kind of people who built it and maintain it are not. They are in every community across the country and can be brought together through the local boards and clinics like this one.

The total operating cost of the Neighborhood Christian Clinic is around $1.5 million annually. While the overhead is low—about $180,000 for administrative and fundraising expenses—the annual cost to see and treat patients currently exceeds $1.3 million. The amount of revenue generated from the patients last year was only $341,000. The rest of the clinic's operating cost, more than $1 million a year, is paid for through donations.

Most clinics and hospitals across the country operate in part because of private sector donations. The boards and auxiliary organizations that operate these not-for-profit institutions are almost always made up of extraordinary volunteers supporting professional management, supplemented by professional staffs who are, in turn, supported by volunteers doing everything from the gift shop sales and candy-striper flower deliveries to surgeries. Skeptics will scoff at the idea that public health centers of excellence can be built and sustained through a model of up-front taxpayer-funded construction spending and a public endowment followed by private donations and volunteer oversight, along with some combination of staff and volunteers. But that is exactly what works in Phoenix and can work elsewhere. The left will complain it is not a comprehensive approach but it is an effective approach to actually delivering heath care to the poorest of the poor, and to communities where health insurance means nothing because deductibles are too high or Medicaid-accepting doctors too rare. The perfect must never be the enemy of the good, especially when the perfect never existed or will never exist in the first place.

The state of Arizona has a program that allows its taxpayers to receive a dollar-for-dollar charitable tax credit up to $800. Instead of sending the money to the state coffers, the taxpayer can send it to the charity of their choice. The credit just expanded under Governor Doug Ducey and his GOP legislative majorities, and that makes it even more advantageous than ever to partner with the mission of restoring health and restoring lives in Phoenix. You don't have to be an Arizona resident to contribute (but you do need to be an Arizona taxpayer to claim the tax credit). You can donate from their website: www.thechristianclinic.org.

More to the point, it is clinics like this one that could spread with help from a Trump infrastructure program.

If TPRM sets its sights on getting clinics like this one up and running in the major urban centers of America, they will have worked a revolution in the delivery of actual health care, and it won't be health care on paper, the way much of Obamacare has turned out to be. It will be the real deal: actual medicine for the people least likely to be able to afford it.

Note that everything I have described above from both Orange County and Phoenix is relatively inexpensive, homegrown, and, crucially, has a physical home—a presence in the community, an address. The actual blueprints for dental clinics, medical clinics, swimming pools, fitness centers, family shelters for the suddenly homeless and transitional housing for those on the rebound are out there. If President Trump and the Speaker and the majority leader want to leave a mark—want to collect those T3s, those "tangible Trump trophies"—they will block-grant large sums to the new county-based boards appointed in conjunction with the president and the Speaker and the leader (the patronage!) and limit their expenditures to 50 percent of the grant and force the rest of the money to serve as a permanent operating expenses endowment.

It would establish Donald Trump and his colleagues

as savvy humanitarians even as it helps launch a political revolution, and would do much to erase the aftereffects of a campaign waged against immigration. The infrastructure investments are part one of the package but its rhetorical positioning is so powerful as to define his presidency at home even as Obamacare defined President Obama's tenure. And these clinics and pools can be authorized and funded by April, under construction by fall and open by next year. Make the money available and put a deadline on using it and the local authorities will make it happen.

This is a mixture of George H. W. Bush's "1,000 Points of Light," which honored the not-for-profits that change lives, and the stimulus bill that squandered $831 billion. It is a politically potent and ideologically compelling innovation of government that moves federal money immediately to local control without either state or federal bureaucrats intervening to drain off resources or distort local need. And it came from the brain of Meathead. What's not to like?

And of course the political payoff is there as well: Set up county commissions to spend their money, naming a majority of members on each from the president (say five), with the Speaker and the majority leader getting two each. Give them lots of leeway and only general guidelines. Some will explode. Some will explore forever. But the vast majority will quickly move to build and endow lasting infrastructure. And cut out the local elected officials and their staffs, with their own agendas and pet projects. Empower new people—successful, private sector professionals and entrepreneurs—to make new investments in new approaches to old, intractable projects.

Infrastructure investment—"tangible Trump trophies"—is only one of the five big components of the "going big" package. The "T-cubed" or "I-cubed"—immediate infrastructure improvements—statutes need to be added to passing tax reform, the military rebuild, the reworking of the courts, and through them the administrative state, and, crucially, unexpectedly, an immigration overhaul.

There are 3,144 counties (or county equivalents, such as "parishes" in Louisiana). It is the ubiquitous unit of government, and the average county population is just slightly more than 100,000. Using that as a "delta"—every 100,000 of population—let's figure that a new county board will get $100 per resident in infrastructure spending, or $10 million for the average county.

In Orange County the Prop 10 commission has spent $538 million over eighteen years and accomplished an amazing amount of infrastructure funding. That works out to $30 million a year of unrestricted funding for a county of 3 million people. So I can say with certainty that great infrastructure strides can be made at about $10 per resident per year in spending over eighteen years, but the average federal block grant for infrastructure to a county shouldn't be a million bucks ($10 per resident in the average county). Rather, it should be ten times that amount—$100 per resident—so that the new boards have endowments from which to draw every year on interest income as well as a mandate to spend the initial block grant down to zero within five years. Like the John M. Olin Foundation and many other foundations, these new county boards should be on a steep descent to a wind-down. The Philanthropy Roundtable summarized Olin's experience:

> The John M. Olin Foundation closed its doors in 2005, 23 years after the death of its founder. Olin carefully selected his staff and board members and instructed the foundation's trustees to disburse its assets over their lifetimes. The Olin Foundation was the crucial early funder of the Federalist Society, and its funding launched a flourishing field in law and economics at leading law schools. Its commitment to sunsetting enabled Olin to achieve a level of grantmaking comparable to foundations three to four times its asset size. Observers on both right and left acknowledge that compared to what a perpetual foundation would have trickled out, Olin's grantmaking strategy and accelerated disbursements significantly strengthened the conservative policy network.

With 3,144 boards of nine people each pushing out grants and then permanent endowments to organizations that use the first and second round of grants in accordance with the general guidelines propounded by the Congress and the president, we will watch a conservative revolution in infrastructure spending. Total cost? One hundred dollars times 330 million Americans: $33 billion of the suggested $83 billion in infrastructure appropriations made early in 2017. That's $33 billion spread out across the land via the new local boards composed of local citizens acting within the loosest of guidelines funding the construction of tangible Trump trophies just as the WPA did, but also endowing their long-term operation—an operation independent of bureaucracies and federal oversight. (Yes, that leaves $50 billion unspent. More on that below.)

Just to make sure even the Pittsburgh Steelers fans get it, I will illustrate how to block-grant the infrastructure dollars using Allegheny County, home to the city that blights the NFL. (I'm a Browns fan.)

There are about 1,230,000 residents in this western Pennsylvania county. So an infrastructure spending bill pegging the endowment to $100 per county would send $123,000,000 to the new nine-member board appointed by the president, the Speaker, and the majority leader. Hopefully they'd put a Rooney on there, a couple of doctors and hospital administrators, some leading public-minded citizens, and a savvy Yinzer journalist like Salena Zito, for example. TPRM will have their networks working and since these jobs don't pay, aren't permanent, and shouldn't come with any benefits save insurance against lawsuits, most applicants will be public-spirited. Those nine will have to hire some staff just as Orange County's Prop 10 commission did, but overhead should be low and lawyering can be done by outside firms. Our commission has the grant forms on file, developed over eighteen years. Again, none of this is new. And none of it needs a single federal bureaucrat. It needs a federal statute and an appropriation.

They'd be told by the new law and the new president: "Spend twenty percent on construction projects within six months—dental and medical clinics, pools, hockey rinks—whatever makes poor kids and their families healthier and fitter—and then go about endowing those programs and other good programs in the county surrounding them. Be out of business in five years."

These 3,144 county commissions will move fast, will make mistakes, and will have to hire some staff to execute contracts and supervise grants. To repeat: mistakes will be made. *But* crucial infrastructure will get built, endowed or both. There's no reason an existing Y, for example, with plans for a new aquatics center but not enough funds, shouldn't get a big grant to build and operate it in perpetuity. Allegheny County can find nine worthy folks to guide its projects and more than enough projects on which to spend about $24 million in immediate construction dollars and organizations on which to expend the remaining approximately $100 million in endowment funding. Then these good citizens can go away, their work done, but the good work begun by them carrying on—without federal bureaucrats or continuing "oversight" costs that are as unnecessary as they are draining of community initiative and energy.

The Obama stimulus failed to leave a trace because it was done by and for Washington, moved at D.C. speed, and insisted in seeing plans and benchmarks as opposed to trusting good and virtuous citizens to do good and virtuous things quickly. President Obama and his team had forgotten the American tradition of "barn-raising," of selfless acts of community building. It is our genius, as Alexis de Tocqueville remarked early in the nineteenth century.

"Americans of all ages, all conditions, all minds constantly unite," he wrote. "Not only do they have commercial and industrial associations in which all take part, but they also have a thousand other kinds: religious, moral, grave, futile, very general and very particular, immense and very small; Americans use associations to give fêtes, to found seminaries, to build inns, to raise churches, to distribute books, to send missionaries to the antipodes; in this manner they create hospitals, prisons, schools. Finally, if it is a question of bringing to light a truth or developing a sentiment with the support of a great example, they associate. Everywhere that, at the head of a new undertaking, you see the government in France and a great lord in England, count on it that you will perceive in association in the United States.

"In America I encountered sorts of associations of which, I confess, I had no idea, and I often admired the infinite art with which the inhabitants of the United States managed to fix a common goal to the efforts of many men and to get them to advance to it freely."

Everywhere in this country there are projects that need doing, clinics that need opening and doctors who need a place to volunteer as they do in Phoenix, parents of special needs children who need services and a place to collect and compare strategies and challenges, and sports teams waiting to spring into being once given a place to swim or run. TPRM can do this. They can. It requires trust in the ordinary citizens far from D.C. who have no desire for a paycheck or a D.C. address.

Keep in mind as the new Congress works with the new president that we have not always needed vast federal bureaucracies watching over vast state bureaucracies watching over professionalized cities where legions of paid staff superintend all decisions. We used to believe in short, clearly written laws and in the good faith of most citizens. Thus the Homestead Act of 1862 is my key example of the Fourth Way as it appeared in the past and as I hope it appears again.

Signed into law in May 1862, the Homestead Act opened up settlement in the western United States, allowing any American, including freed slaves, to put in a claim for up to 160 free acres of federal land. By the end of the Civil War, 15,000 homestead claims had been registered and the rush west continued. Eventually 1.6 million individual claims would be approved, with more than 400,000 square miles of federal land conferred very easily on private citizens.

The Homestead Act of 1862 was four handwritten pages long. I reproduce it in the Appendix in its entirety to show that vast things can be accomplished with very short laws and with only a small federal bureaucracy to watch it being carried out.

Sure, there was a General Land Office—established in 1812 in the Department of the Treasury and moved in 1849 to the Department of the Interior, and today known as the Bureau of Land Management. And, sure, the General Land Office was authorized by this short 1862 law "to prepare and issue such rules and regulations, consistent with this act, as shall be necessary and proper to carry its provisions into effect." But the Land Office's size was tiny compared to the vast bureaucracies of today, and its mission specific and executed quickly. Today's BLM has about 10,000 employees. I cannot find a source for the number of the employees in the General Land Office in 1862, but the Census Bureau had a grand total of 182 staff in 1860, so it is a fair guess that the Homestead Act was executed with very little supervision and a whole lot of hurry on the part of very few federal employees. And the land was settled. Lots got done.

This can be done again today. The "Immediate Infrastructure Improvements Act" can be every bit as short—I could write it in a day—and a parallel law with a parallel structure and appropriation for airports and ports could be done the same way. (Recall there's another $50 billion in new stimulus to invest.) The Fourth Way. And renewal would follow, rapidly, effectively, transparently. "It is a truth as important as it is agreeable," wrote Secretary of the Treasury Alexander Hamilton in his 1791 *Report on The Subject of Manufactures,* "and one to which it is not easy to find exceptions, that everything tending to establish substantial and permanent order in the affairs of a country, to increase the total mass of industry and opulence, is ultimately beneficial to every part of it."

Do well by the poorest parts of the country and the country will do well, if Hamilton is to be believed. And Hamilton is much, much more than a Broadway hit. Hamilton is the father of the Fourth Way. He passionately believed in infrastructure improvements, as did a young Illinois congressman who in 1848 argued for them on the floor of the House.

"Congress should establish a list of projects that met the test of national advantage, even if indirectly," Abraham Lincoln argued from the floor, "the way the Illinois–Michigan canal benefits New Orleans as well as New York and every place between."

Lincoln's faith in "infrastructure"—"internal improvements" they were called then—was near complete, no matter how they were constructed. Now of course we don't need canals or steamboat docks any more than we need Carnegie libraries. We need health care and fitness facilities, homeless shelters and transitional housing, and, yes, airport expansions and new port facilities. We especially need shipyards, as will be discussed in the chapter on defense.

But for immediate pop in the populations most in need of it, follow the model of the Prop 10 commissions, especially Orange County's.

"[I]f the nation refuse to make improvements, of the more general kind, because their benefits may be somewhat local, a state may, for the same reason, refuse to make an improvement of a local kind, because its benefits may be somewhat general," Lincoln argued. "A state may well say to the nation 'If you will do nothing for me, I will do nothing for you.' Thus it is seen, that if this argument of 'inequality' is sufficient any where, it is sufficient every where; and puts an end to improvements altogether.

"I hope and believe," Lincoln concluded, "that if both the nation and states would, in good faith, in their respective spheres, do what they could in the way of improvements, what of inequality might be produced in one place, might be compensated in another, and that the sum of the whole might not be very unequal."

Thus would infrastructure investments in the poorest communities redound to the benefit of every American. And those improvements could be married to the biggest, most breathtaking move of all.

As Nixon Went to China, So Trump Can Orchestrate an Immigration Overhaul

When it comes to actually proposing, passing, and implementing an immigration overhaul, the "key of we" will be most unexpected and most difficult to hit and maintain.

But Donald J. Trump can do what perhaps no other American politician can do: he can reform the immigration system while regularizing the 11 million immigrants in the country without permission and while also building a "wall"—in reality a long, strong, double-row border fence with an interstate running between the two fences for the Border Patrol to travel on quickly. He can do this without any credible number of serious critics branding it an "amnesty" or a "sellout."

Trump can do a "Nixon to China" with an immigration overhaul. In fact he may be the individual with the last, best chance to get this done. And paired with the infrastructure above and the initiatives of conservative orthodoxy that follow, he can have it done by June 2017, accomplishing in half a year what President Obama could not do in eight (as well as securing the nascent political realignment President Trump began, away from an American version of European socialism).

To repeat: President Trump can hit "the key of we" on immigration and in so doing stun his critics and secure his place in history.

We begin with the simple fact that if Donald Trump is for an immigration overhaul, whatever its components, any attempt to brand it as an amnesty will fail, just as the efforts to brand Nixon as "soft on Mao" failed forty-plus years ago.

When the credentials on a controversial subject are established beyond argument, no argument overcomes the credentials.

If President Trump pronounces himself satisfied with a package on immigration, even if it amnesty (and it won't be), it will be passed and it will be accepted by the right. If he grabs this particular "third rail"—there are many third rails in American politics—he will electrify American politics. And he will guarantee himself and his party a governing majority for as far as the eye can see.

The specifics of a "good deal" on immigration have been hiding in plain sight for a decade, but Republicans afraid of their base, have alternated between hesitation and bad compromises, and Democrats have not minded the political sufferings that have befallen the GOP as a result of its series of perfectly executed half maneuvers that left it exposed to withering political crossfire. Gridlock and political losses for the GOP as well as paralysis on key reforms have been the result.

President Trump can smash the gridlock. He can secure lasting political realignment along the way.

Having proposed spending to benefit lower-income communities across the country with infrastructure initiatives, President Trump can cut the Gordian knot on immigration by having his engineering team lay out the fencing plans in great detail, and then mandate that upon its completion (or 50 or 75 percent of its completion) all law-abiding immigrants shall be regularized and permitted to stay in the United States with a new "purple card," but of course not allowed to become citizens unless and until they return to the countries of their birth to stand in line with everyone else. With this package of measures he hits a political grand slam. Everybody wins.

The objections are easily anticipated and answered.

Why not let the regularized vote? Because they entered the country illegally. Would-be citizens ought not to begin a journey to citizenship with an act of lawlessness.

Why let the small percentage of immigrants in the country illegally who are convicted criminals or known gang members stay? Didn't you see the part about "law abiding"? They shouldn't be.

The Department of Homeland Security, some will object, can't handle 11 million applications! True, which is why President Trump should ask Congress to authorize him to establish "regularization" panels in each county that can hand out purple cards upon a reasonable showing of an immigrant's good record and good prospects. Populate these panels with retired military officers—professional assessors of talent and character, all of whom have dealt with people of all backgrounds—and the job gets done in a hurry. Retired officers have completed or reviewed hundreds if not thousands of "fitness reports." They are skilled readers of personnel files, hearers of stories, assessors of claims. Using the county structure even as draft boards once did, regularization panels in every county can simply invite the would-be purple card recipients to appear with their files, including their best-case statements, their paid bills, the evidence of where they have been and what they have done, and issue decisions. Stay or not. Families intact. Productive people hurried along to regularized status. Sketchy applications studied more intently, referred to law enforcement for assistance, but with a strong presumption that they be allowed to stay and thrive. No benefits for the purple card holders that are not paid for by their state or local governments, but access to education of course. The message will be sent: "You are forgiven your trespass and welcome to stay, you and your families, but if you want to vote you will have to go home and get in the long line."

After a couple of years of processing, employers will be expected to insist on proof of legal residence, or suffer extraordinary penalties. Problem solved. Message sent.

And the fence too will send a message. Understand that seven hundred miles of "fencing" was authorized a decade ago in one of the Dean Martin Republicans' series of failed efforts to entertain their base instead of solving the problem. Most of the authorized fencing was never built. A lot of what was built were traffic barriers easily walked over. Some of it was transparently absurd "virtual" fencing that always runs into a bad comparison with the "real fencing" that surrounds the White House or cuts through the West Bank and which is being constructed as fast as can be done in various Middle East and European countries. "Virtual" is not what Americans want. They want the real deal: tall, double rowed, with a paved road between them so that Border Patrol vehicles can speedily, well, patrol. And apprehend and return fence jumpers.

(An aside: Nonserious people say fourteen-foot fences mean fifteen-foot ladders. Yeah, right. Think it through. Even where some very crafty "coyotes" manage to move not one but two or three fifteen-foot ladders to a fence crossing point, can't everyone just admit that the immediate consequence of a completed double row of fifteen-foot fences will be to cut illegal border crossing by nearly 100 percent? People are not stupid. Signal "serious" and border crossers will start giving up. Americans want border security. And long, strong, high double-row border fences with a road in between the two fences is the visible expression of an invisible commitment to border security that they have long demanded and been refused by the Beltway elites.)

The vast majority of Americans are not in the least anti-immigrant and most citizens living in the states most considerably impacted by illegal immigration—California, Arizona, New Mexico, and Texas—live close to and daily work with some who are not in the country lawfully and think nothing of it and fear regularization not at all. Legal immigrants often resent the idea of an "Olly olly oxen free!" path to the citizenship that they had to work hard to secure. But even this group should not object to a noncitizenship regularization of the vast majority of the 11 million who want to get on with their lives.

The fence is the key to the deal, but it is not the whole solution as people will continue to overstay visas and human smugglers will continue to cross waters and get in via our ports.

But the big deal that President Trump can get done is right before our collective eyes. Paired with the infrastructure spending it will leave his harshest critics sputtering.

And the 29 percent of the Hispanic population that voted for him? It will soar beyond the 42 percent that George W. Bush achieved.

The payoffs are too great for President Trump not to deploy an infrastructure and immigration bill to launch his presidency. The deal is there for the taking. And concurrent with its razzle and dazzle must come the delivery of another promise: the rebuilding of the American military.

About That "Other" $50 Billion

If I had my way, I'd spend every dollar of infrastructure through the Trump boards, thus putting federalism and subsidiarity on steroids, and turn the 100 pools into 1,000 aquatics centers. But Congress is going to be Congress and pork is gonna be pork. Thus I'd take half that amount—$25 billion—and put it directly into the hands of every representative or senator who votes affirmatively for the overall package of infrastructure spending, immigration overhaul, defense spending, and tax reform package to use for projects within their district or state as they see fit, as long as it is spent on funding endowments for existing not-for-profits within the year and as long as it is done transparently. That's about $50 million per representative and senator. They can't mess up endowment spending too much, and they will end up again bypassing bureaucrats and get the money into the hands of the little platoons of virtue throughout their states and districts. Ask a congressman what they would do with this, and their eyes will light up. They are elected representatives; they know who gets what done. And transparency and speed means a minimum of corruption. (There will be some. There always is.)

And conditioning receipt of the funds upon an affirmative vote? That's just good politics (and an idea I owe to Grant Starrett, whom I hope will someday be elected to office).

Of the other $25 billion? Into the capable hands of Secretary of Transportation Elaine Chao for her—and only her—direction to the ports and airports that can show immediate need for new actual facilities. This would free Democrats of the fear that President Trump will be directing dollars to friends and away from enemies (though what is much of federal spending over its two-plus centuries except that very thing?). President Trump spent quite a lot of time talking on the campaign trail about the need for airport and port improvements and he is right. These are the facilities of growth. Injecting capital into them is a fine thing. The Homestead Act of 1862 was four pages. The airports and ports infrastructure portion of the Immediate Infrastructure Improvement Act of 2017 should be four paragraphs. We need to especially learn from Lincoln—the man behind the Homestead Act, the Second Inaugural, and the Gettysburg Address—and from the Constitution's Framers that length is no substitute for clarity and purpose. The out-of-control administrative state thrives on tens of thousands of pages of fine print and hundreds of pages of unread legislation. The cure is judgment empowered by brevity in law.

Throughout this chapter there are themes of the

Fourth Way: Trust local people. Don't trust or enrich federal or state bureaucracies or even a permanent local bureaucracy. Transparency. Accountability. And above all, speed. Speed doesn't kill; it powers the Trump boom, even as the Trump immigration overhaul will shock tax receipts in a positive enduring way as the shadow economy comes into the open.

All of this is possible, and more, provided the country also attends to the spending it needs to reinvigorate and expand its military, to which we turn next.

III

The New and Renewed American Military

On October 21, 2016, President Trump made these commitments:

> We are also going to rebuild our badly depleted military.
>
> Our Navy is the smallest it's been since World War I. My plan will build the 350-ship Navy we need. This will be the largest effort at rebuilding our military since Ronald Reagan, and it will require a truly national effort. The Philadelphia Navy Yard is a perfect example. I will instruct my secretary of the Navy to study locations like Philadelphia with a long history of service to our military and proximity to vibrant private industry and find ways to involve them in this national effort.
>
> As our fleet is rebuilt, we'll need to invest in recruiting the skilled American craftsmen we need, like welders and pipefitters and so much more.
>
> We will establish "centers of excellence" in

> places like Philadelphia and Portsmouth, New Hampshire, and Hampton Roads in Virginia to produce the master craftsmen we need to rebuild our fleet.
>
> We will rebuild our Navy and we will do it with American steel made right here in Pennsylvania.

And, President Trump, might have added, "and in every state in what was once part of the blue wall but which voted for me because they knew the jobs that go with rebuilding America's depleted military will be spread throughout the industrial centers that powered our growth in the last century, and which won the Second World War and indeed the Cold War."

There are pressing capitalization needs across all branches of the U.S. military, but if President Trump insists on this single goal of 350 ships in the fleet, the backbone of a revitalized American military will be in place. There are many paths to 350 ships and the cost is enormous but the benefits—to national security, to the American economy, and to international stability—are enormous as well. That's because the fleet is the visible expression of American will to lead the free world and its missions are many and crucial. How to get there?

I have consulted four experts on the Navy and the Marine Corps in laying out the various paths: Robert C. O'Brien—a close friend, law partner, and senior national security adviser to, among others, former GOP nominee Mitt Romney, Governor Scott Walker, and Senator Ted Cruz; retired Navy Captain Jerry Hendrix, now at the Center for a New American Security; "Officer X," a senior acquisitions specialist with deep knowledge of current infrastructure and supply chain capabilities and limitations; and Major General Mel Spiese (USMC, Ret.), a longtime friend and an extraordinarily accomplished military professional.

I asked each to give me a path and three of their very specific sets of instructions are included in Appendix B. I have done this to prove that plans for rebuilding the military are not the product of a civilian who has read too many Tom Clancy novels for his own good, or of insulated think-tankers with dreams built out of talking points. These proposals meet real needs identified by professionals who have spent their lives in uniform (or, in the case of O'Brien, both in uniform and as a national security expert and international lawyer). What you will find in Appendix B are options for the Navy and a specific listing of what the Marine Corps needs and why we need the Marine Corps. What matters most is that the Congress work quickly with the new president to draw on such outlines—and there are others but these are plausible, professional examples of what needs to be done and blueprints on how to do it—and to establish a plan, authorize it, and secure the spending and the schedule necessary to make it a reality.

There are many possible paths to a 350-ship Navy

and a fully supplied and ready USMC. President-elect Trump has to oversee the fashioning of one plan to propose to the Congress—after expedited consultations with senior DOD military, civilian officials, and private sector experts—and Congress has to refine and adopt.

There really isn't a debate here on need or the threat we face. No serious defense analyst disagrees. One only needs to look at the rapidly growing Chinese navy and the People's Republic of China (PRC)'s aggressive assertion of sovereignty over the South China Sea to understand that the era of unchallenged U.S. naval supremacy is behind us. A complete picture of the threats is available in Robert C. O'Brien's 2016 book, *While America Slept*, which I recommend as a supplement to this book and specifically to this chapter. The key points though:

- By 2020 or even sooner, the PRC could have a navy larger than the U.S. Navy (USN) in the Pacific, and at least 140 of its ships will be modern and multi-mission capable.
- The People's Liberation Army (PLA) navy will be "missile centric," with its ships bristling with antiship missiles aimed at defeating U.S. carrier battle groups.
- The PLA navy will likely have more submarines than the USN, which is a deadly advantage and an astonishing fact to most casual observers who had assumed that America's undersea dominance was our country's and the USN's top priority.

Though it is in the South China Sea that the PRC's strategy of using weapons or vessels to prevent an adversary from occupying or traversing an area has been carried out the most so far, the Middle Kingdom intends to be an even more significant global force than it is already, and it is establishing bases to make it so. The land-based Dong Feng 21D antiship missile, currently in early stages of development, will, when deployed, be able to threaten our Navy and allied ships from a distance of 1,500 kilometers.

- The PRC only has a single aircraft carrier now, but the construction of four more is planned. As is the expansion of the PRC's own fleet of "boomers" (naval slang for ballistic missile submarines, which are armed with nuclear warheads), the "Type 094" Jin class sub.

Neither the PRC nor Russia is going to call off its plans to build ships and expand naval forces. Far from it. They saw their opening in the Obama-era scale-back of the U.S. Navy and they have taken it.

The United States presently has 282 active-duty ships, give or take a few depending on how one counts. The "best-case" Obama-era building plan would have topped out at 321, but even that modest expansion is in doubt with the ruinous sequester in place. Those are the automatic across-the-board cuts that go into place if the executive and legislative branches can't agree to restrain the budget by a certain deadline.

The real need? The National Defense Panel report on the 2014 Quadrennial Defense Review called for a minimum 323–346 ship Navy (not anywhere near the number actually planned for in the Obama era). And specialists concluded in the same report that to actually meet 100 percent of the current combatant commanders' requirements for naval forces to support U.S. missions around the globe, the number of ships should be 450.

President Trump put down a realistic goal of 350 ships, not the needed 450. We do have allies and they do have fleets and obligations to expand them as well. But how to get to the 350? And what is the right ship mix?

I have read the various scenarios proposed and include three in the Appendix, but the key is that Chairman of the Joint Chiefs of Staff General Joe Dunford, Chief of Naval Operations Admiral John Richardson, and Commandant of the Marine Corps Lieutenant General Robert Neller need to lead an expedited effort to put forward the Pentagon's preferred approach and then civilian leaders need to review and refine it—and commit to it. That review will no doubt stress the expedited production of the SSBX-class nuclear submarine—the new "boomer" that will gradually replace our aging Ohio class. But much more is needed, including a plan to renew our carrier fleet and the ships to support the battle groups that cruise alongside the carriers.

It can be done. But don't believe me; believe the four experts I consulted immediately after the election.

I asked people like Robert O'Brien, Captain Hendrix, Officer X, and General Spiese for their views to make sure this book deals with specifics and realities, not pie-in-the-sky think-tankery. Getting the fleet to 350 and the USMC recharged are doable, and quickly.

I sought out the experts included here to underscore the fact that this kind of knowledge doesn't have to come from Capitol Hill or the federal agencies. The best new thinking comes from the outside, where lobbyists and industry haven't been working the referees on the Hill. The Pentagon's expertise is invaluable, but the Hill's, not so much. There are some electeds, like Senators Lindsey Graham and Tom Cotton, with whom the new president ought to sit down, and some members of the House Armed Services Committee as well, but President Trump would be well served by gathering twenty of the best, including my four, into a room where the meetings are run by him and then charging Vice President Pence and the task force with instructions to come out with a plan in two weeks. Then he should review, approve, send that plan to the Hill and fight it out, and then make it into a strategic document that will decide our goals in terms of military strength for each of the next twenty years. And we should build many of those ships in reopened old shipyards, or new shipyards located in areas passed over by globalization. The Great Lakes shoreline is full of potential locations for the industrial base that could be revitalized by servicing a 350-ship Navy. "Industrial policy" is a dangerous concept if carried too far into the details of the free market's operation, but sighting and funding expansion of the industrial base that can design, build, and maintain the fleet is one area where the federal government can and should play a large role, if only because of the strategic needs involved.

There are other easily articulated goals. They include an Army with a strength of 540,000, an Air Force of at least 1,200 active fighter aircraft, and more cyberwarfare forces spread out across the Department of Defense (DOD). Our missile defense system also needs to be reenergized quickly given the growing threats from rogue states and nonstate actors. And of course we need an intelligence community with vastly expanded numbers of human actors.

But it all begins with the Navy and the Marine Corps. And with a plan. And with a commitment to stick to the plan for as long as President Trump is in office—and beyond. In the new world of near-peer and soon-to-be-peer competitors, the United States can never take another "holiday from history," as it has now twice in the sixteen years of the Obama and Clinton presidencies.

As for those thoughts on where to build those ships and how to pay for them, see part V. But first, a focus on the federal courts.

IV

A Supreme Court and Federal Judiciary That Umpires, Not Plays

Stagger is an overused word, but properly employed it ought to refer to those rare occasions when a country or individual is physically or almost physically thrown back by his or her own body against a wall or to the floor because of the emotional impact of an event.

Parents losing children—the greatest grief—are staggered. Losing a parent, spouse, or the closest of friends can stagger. The United States was collectively staggered by 9/11 and then repeatedly by the financial blows and collapses of the panic of 2008.

It is rare when an injury to or death of a nonrelative or close friend can stagger you but it has happened to me three times. I was a first-year law student at the University of Michigan in 1981 when two of those three events happened: the assassination attempt on President Reagan on March 30, 1981, and the shooting of Pope John Paul II just weeks later, on May 13. Both attempts at the murder of leaders I had come to admire as keys to the future knocked me back. I can recall leaning against a wall in Hutchins Hall at the law school when someone told me the pope had been shot. You recoil from such acts of pure evil and then you recover, pray for the victim, and press on. Both men survived.

The third occasion came when United States Supreme Court Justice Antonin Scalia died unexpectedly on the night of February 12 or the early morning of February 13, 2016. I did not know the justice except for a brief time in the fall of 1983 when the judge for whom I was clerking, Roger Robb, of the U.S. Court of Appeals for the D.C. Circuit, became ill. As a result, his two clerks, Terry Ross and me, were "adopted" by the entire bench and were given cases by a few of the judges, including Judge Scalia and his friend then Judge Ruth Bader Ginsburg, until Judge George MacKinnon took us in on a permanent basis. Judge Scalia as a younger man was exactly the fellow you would expect: concerned but also focused on giving Ross and me a chance to do what judicial clerks do—learn while working the back rooms and the library. He was very kind, ebullient, and brilliant.

The whole country came to know Scalia, at least those parts that care about court cases that roll out to touch millions of lives for the precedents they set. When he ascended to the United States Supreme Court he became the godfather of "originalism," the school of judicial thought that stressed fealty to the design of the Framers and that embraced the view that the document was what it was: a self-contained set of rules for how the United States was to operate, a carefully balanced set of checks and balances, a federal government of three independent and equal branches holding each other at bay and in check, a system of federalism that understood the states as coequal sovereigns within their realms, and a set of amendments that limited what either the federal or state governments could do vis-à-vis individual citizens. A government of limited, enumerated powers, and a judiciary designed to patrol those boundaries of power in a straightforward fashion.

Of course, how "originalism" works to keep the powers balanced and liberty thriving is open to ongoing dispute. But Justice Scalia was its champion, and by far its most brilliant exponent, a writer of fierce ability rounded at the edges by a fierce sense of humor. Justice Scalia was a genuine "lion of the law," and his opinions, especially his dissents, have received a lot of emphasis in the constitutional law classes I have taught at the Fowler School of Law at Chapman University in Orange, California, since its doors opened in 1995. In a closely divided Court—a Court that includes four "living Constitution" enthusiasts, four "originalists," and Justice Anthony Kennedy moving between the camps—Justice Scalia was always a lighthouse for the people who believed and still believe that the Framers were a unique collection of geniuses. And while their collective work included horrible flaws that needed correction through amendments, including the one that eradicated slavery after a horrific civil war, the original design of the parts not having to do with slavery needs to be faithfully applied and defended, and amendments need to be constitutionally enacted.

Whatever our disagreements with his decisions, originalists like me admired Justice Scalia as our preeminent voice and authority, , as one who believed in the Constitution's delicate balance, with a long record of supporting the incremental, ongoing expansion of liberty and literacy at home, as well as of the president's authority to superintend America's role abroad to pursue the same goals.

Thus when he died suddenly, on the cusp on an election that would decide so much, originalists like me were thrown back. We had wrongly assumed that the Court's aging contingent would go on and on, split down the middle for at least as long as it would take for a Republican president to return and appoint able successors to retiring "conservatives" and thus preserve the delicate balance or perhaps even tilt it back to originalism.

This debate—originalism versus the "living Constitution"—is at the heart of the relief many conservatives found in the triumph of President Trump. No one believes that President Trump is much concerned with the particulars of any set of cases or line of precedents, or even with the Supreme Court's work as a whole. But most of us who are concerned with all of those things trust his commitment on his first nomination to the Supreme Court specifically and subsequent appointments generally, and for reasons I will discuss below. First, though, for the laymen, why do these appointments mean so much in the long term?

On September 15, 2011, Associate Justice Stephen Breyer, one of the "liberals" on the Court and a great gentleman and scholar, came to my radio studio in California to discuss his new book, *Making Democracy Work*. We spent an hour in genuine conversation that, while respecting the rules that justices don't talk politics or pending cases, remains—I believe—the most candid debate between a "living Constitution" sitting justice and a critic not on the Court. I recommend the whole of it to you, but these closing exchanges tease out the fundamental difference between us, and between the two schools:

Hugh Hewitt: Mr. Justice Breyer, when we went to break, you were talking about the need for civic education. I one hundred percent agree. I go out, and I talk at high schools. I teach my Con Law. . . .

Justice Stephen Breyer: Good.

HH: Everyone should be doing that. But I always teach them as well, realism. And the realism that stands before me today is a Court that just, it is unpredictable, the Constitution is whatever five justices say. Five of them say *Citizens United* means that *Austin* should be overturned. Five of them say abortion should be legal in fifty states. Five of them say Bush, four of them say Gore, that it really is, the realist says it's whatever five justices of the Court say the Constitution is. How do you answer that to the people listening and believe it?

Justice Breyer: Oh, I'm not a realist. I mean, I don't think it just is politics. And I spend a lot of time trying to explain why it just can't be politics. And there are different people who have different views, but the job of a judge there is to try to figure out the answer to this legal question. I mean, some people think the answers are all found in history. Justice Scalia says that's originalism. And the motive of that is a good motive, because I think that they want to control the subjective influence of the judge. They think that what I do, for example, or by looking more to congressional purposes, or trying to figure out what the values are underlying, say, the freedom of speech, underlying parts of the Constitution. They think it's too subjective. I don't think it's too subjective. I think I write down my reasons, and I think people are free to criticize them, and you have. There's nothing wrong with that. We're used to criticism. And that's fine. People certainly can criticize and pay attention to it in general. Of course they can criticize. But there are different approaches to these very grand problems, very different. And I think, for example, originalism doesn't work very well. I think it's pretty hard. I don't think George Washington knew about the Internet. I think our basic job there is to take the values in the Constitution, which don't change. They're virtually the same now as they were in the eighteenth century. They're the values of the Enlightenment, and apply them to today's world which changes every five minutes. I mean, yes, George Washington didn't know the Internet, nor did James Madison know about television, et cetera. And this world keeps changing.

HH: They knew liberty. That's what they knew. They knew liberty.

Justice Breyer: Correct.

HH: Let me give you my favorite approach to the Constitution.

Justice Breyer: All right.

HH: It's from the Massachusetts ratification convention, January 25th, 1788. Mr. Smith rises up and says, "Mr. President, I am a plain man, and I get my living by the plow. I'm not used to speaking in public, but I beg your leave to say a few words to my brother plow joggers in this house." And he goes on to say, "When I saw this Constitution, I found that it was a cure for these disorders. It was just such a thing as wanted. I got a copy of it and read it over and over. I had been a member of the convention to form our own state constitution, and learnt something of the checks and balances of power, and I found them all there, and I did not go to any lawyer to ask his opinion. We have no lawyers in our town, and we do well enough without. I form my own opinion, and I'm pleased with this Constitution." There is the democratic impulse. And I think that the courts are at war with it, not the Supreme Court always and exclusively, but courts across the United States issuing these thunderbolts on marriage, and on all sorts of different social hot-button issues, when the people haven't. . . . They're ahead of the people, Mr. Justice. Do you understand what the concern is from that point?

Justice Breyer: I do understand the concern. And the difficulty is that for eighty years in the United States, we had a system of legal racial segregation.

HH: But that was after the Fourteenth Amendment.

Justice Breyer: So where . . . ah, yeah, yeah. Where was Mr. Smith at that moment? I mean, if he had read that Constitution, he would say that it forbids this racial segregation. But it wasn't happening. And the reason that Hamilton and Madison and the others wanted the Court, courts in general, people have arguments, don't they? And they need to have them decided. As far as the Supreme Court is concerned, they thought it would be important, even though they're risking error, to have a group of people who are trained as lawyers, at least, and to try to keep the others in bounds. And you say oh, the others will stay in bounds naturally. What about those eighty years of racial segregation? Go look at those pictures of how black children in the South were educated. Look at those shacks. Look at the two drinking fountains. Look at the segregated transport. And it was long, hard effort by a lot of people, not just the courts, but the courts included, to try to bring the country into correspondence with the Constitution. And so it isn't true, you see, to say they're just sitting there causing trouble. What they're doing, in fact, is trying to make those ideals, and the ideals aren't totally liberty, the ideals are how to create a workable government that as a practical matter will ensure people both their freedom, and the right for them, themselves, through democracy and the ballot box, to decide what kind of country they want. That's a very complicated effort. And that's the effort of the Court, to assure that reality corresponds to the ideals that are written in the document. And I do want people to understand the difficulty of the task, to understand that we might be wrong, to understand the need for protection of unpopular people, among other things, and then to say I see. You see, I believe on hope that the more understanding that there is, the more support there will be for our constitutional institutions, including the courts.

HH: But to earn that, when the Fourteenth Amendment, as a member of the party of Lincoln, the Civil War is fought, and the Fourteenth Amendment is passed, and it addresses racial, the evil of racial discrimination, and it amends the Constitution the way it needs to be amended. That is very different for the Court to then come in with that predicate and say you are not true to what this six hundred thousand people were killed for in the Civil War. We are going to enforce the decree of the Civil War. Very different when there's not a constitutional amendment on something like, for example, whether or not the Fourteenth Amendment extends to sexual orientation, or whether or not the Fourteenth Amendment guarantees this or that. And so I think it kind of sidesteps the point, almost, to say racial, the Court's greatest moment, *Brown v. Board,* does not give them a writ to go about and invent for themselves this Fourteenth Amendment rationale.

Justice Breyer: You know what I think is the worst moment? The worst moment was the *Dred Scott* decision.

HH: Agreed.

Justice Breyer: And it's interesting to read that.

HH: Great, great chapter.

Justice Breyer: And there, they said, yeah, and you read that the Court, I think very wrongly, at the time, without the Thirteenth, Fourteenth, and Fifteenth Amendment, without those amendments, the Court wrongly held that a descendant of a black slave had no rights at all. . . .

HH: . . . Your colleague and friend, Justice Scalia, has often quoted, mentioned Justice Taney's portrait in Harvard Law School looking glum, having blown the *Dred Scott* decision. But doesn't *Dred Scott* act as a great caution on you?

Justice Breyer: Yes.

HH: That you guys can get it so wrong?

Justice Breyer: Yes, and that's how I use it. I mean, what's so interesting about that is, I mean, they virtually, the decision said that the slave is protected in the free territories, and you can't get rid of slavery. I mean, there was an element of that. And they were at great dissent by Benjamin Curtis, who explained why under the law at the time, that was wrong. And if Taney was trying to stop the Civil War, he started it, or certainly helped. And Abraham Lincoln read the *Curtis* dissent, and said this is a great dissent, used it in the Cooper Union speech, got to be the head of the party as a result, was strong in the Republican Party, and history went on from there. All right, I do use it the same way you do, that the Court can make its mistakes, and that's a real killer. That's a terrible mistake. So we all have our favorites. And I think it's universal that was a mistake. But as to a lot of others, some think they're right, some think they're wrong. And that's their right, and there's no answer. And that brings you back to the basic question. Why should there be this unelected institution that will make mistakes, and that will do things that are unpopular? And the answer to that question lies in Hamilton's view. We want to protect those unpopular people, Madison's view, and John Marshall, with *Marbury v. Madison,* and two hundred years of American history, that include President Eisenhower's flying one thousand troops from the 101st Airborne into Little Rock so that those one thousand troops could go and take those nine heroes, the Little Rock Nine, black children, into the white school. All that's part of our history, it has its ups and downs. And my own bet is that when people begin to learn that history, they'll say, I see. I see why we have a room, the courtroom, where people of every race, every religion, every point of view, can try to work out their differences under law, rather than try to work them out on the street with guns or sticks or bats or whatever. And really, this is, I heard Harry Reid say that after *Bush v. Gore,* that the great thing about that case, it's hardly ever remarked, that that under law is how we decided even that controversial kind of case. I mean, I thought we shouldn't have. Remember, I thought it was wrong. Okay, but that's the system we've developed over two hundred years, and I want people to understand it.

There is quite a lot of fencing going on in these two thousand words, and Justice Breyer is a gold medalist at defending his position since his appointment by President Clinton in 1994 and before that on the First Circuit and in the classrooms at Harvard Law School. But the core disagreement between him and my school of thought is right there, and it is about humility and deference—judicial humility and deference to the Article I and Article II branches and the sovereign states from the Article III courts. A humility is what informs originalism and asks justices and judges not to overreach the elected branches and the people or the state governments—or only when the Constitution absolutely demands it. That humility is about deferring instead to the people and to their collective judgments, about letting the country work out its arguments through elections and about avoiding abrupt interventions except when the Constitution's mandate is clear.

Thus the late-nineteenth-century Court, informed by the purposes of the Civil War Amendments, ought never to have first abandoned those purposes in an episode known as the Slaughterhouse Cases. The Supreme Court refused to infuse the Congress with powers given it by those amendments to protect all citizens of all colors and stations against tyrannical state governments. The Court again perverted those purposes in the *Plessy v. Ferguson* decision of 1896, which wrongly upheld the ghastly scar of "separate but equal," a scar that was not addressed squarely until *Brown v. Board of Education* overturned *Plessy* in 1954. In fact, it took decades of cases and the Civil Rights Act of 1964 and the Voting Rights Act of 1965 to fully overrule *Plessy* and another few decades of Court supervision and intervention to start repairing the scar.

The Court needs to act to enforce the Constitution's clear mandates on occasion, and when it doesn't, as with the *Korematsu* decision in 1944 upholding the internment of citizens of Japanese origin, it fails in its central task. But failures—even epic failures like *Korematsu* and *Dred Scott*—did not license the Court to slip the moorings and set sail on its own course, making its own rules.

A lack of deference powered *Roe v. Wade* and the subsequent forty-years war over abortion that the Court didn't settle but only made worse. Instead, we could have had states on their own authority and in their own schedule work out their own laws and thus achieve a national balance. That's what the states were doing on marriage issues when *Obergefell v. Hodges* descended in 2015 as a hammer on the views of the vast majority of states, extending the fundamental right to marry to same-sex couples. Deference was at work in the now obviously genius opinion of Chief Justice Roberts in the Obamacare decision.

A moment on that. Since its issuance I have defended the chief justice's decision as a masterpiece of judicial deference and constitutional balancing. There is an old rule—one of the oldest—that the Supreme Court ought not to strike down a statute unless there is no way to make the case for its constitutional appropriateness. A statute represents the work of two branches, and in the case of Obamacare, the signature achievement of the first African American president working with a mandate represented by a supermajority in the Senate and a heavily Democratic House. The law was a disaster, but it was duly passed by elected representatives and signed into law by a president who had won an enormous victory based in part on the promise of something like it.

Obamacare was a terribly flawed law and its repeal is imminent and necessary. But had the chief justice added his vote to those of the four justices who wanted to strike it down, where would the country be today? Obamacare is a legislative mess about to be addressed by a legislature that has been elected in large part to do away with the mess. The repeal will be legitimate. The striking down of it would have been a lasting blow to the Court. We cannot reimagine history with any certainty, but we can be certain that, if Obamacare had been struck down in the summer of 2010, President Obama would have campaigned against the Court in the fall of 2010 and not instead in defense of his namesake statute, and thus the vast rebuke to him of the 2010 elections would not have been delivered.

In the Obamacare decision, the Chief Justice also showed deference when he sketched out definitive limits on the application of congressional power through the Commerce Clause and Spending Clause. For one, he cemented an understanding of the Commerce Clause that limits Congress to the regulation of commercial activity across state lines. That the taxing power was perhaps stretched is true, but the Court needs to bend toward deference when the issue is close and the other branches united. The chief justice's opinion will soon be taught alongside *Marbury v. Madison* as a brilliant example of judicial power cloaked in judicial humility.

When the Court needs to strike—as with the *Citizens United* and *Hobby Lobby* decisions, which upheld the robust exercise of free speech and the free-exercise rights (the latter protected by the Religious Freedom Restoration Act)—it must do so. It must do so especially when the Bill of Rights is in play, as those amendments were the price of the ratification and their imposition on the states the consequence of the Civil War. There is a path where the Framers' and Lincoln's vision is upheld, and the people are charged to conduct their own affairs within the parameters of the law's highest limits.

Justice Breyer thinks it is a hard thing to find that path. "George Washington didn't know the Internet, nor did James Madison know about television, et cetera," he told me. "And this world keeps changing."

"They knew liberty," I responded. "That's what they knew. They knew liberty."

And justices and judges who know and revere "liberty" and the Constitution's plan to preserve it are what are needed right now. President Trump and Senate Majority Leader McConnell and his caucus and fair-minded Democrats have a chance, unique in my lifetime, to secure that liberty and a Supreme Court majority that honors and upholds the Constitution. A different outcome in the election would have sealed our fate as a nation of citizens only so far as the Supreme Court—and not the Constitution—said we were citizens.

When he was a candidate for the presidency, President Trump released a list of twenty-one candidates from whom he would select his first Supreme Court justice nomination. I include the complete list and a couple of sentences of background on each of them in Appendix C to give you the details if you are interested.

Here's the key, though.

All are qualified. All of them. The youngest of them—Justice Blackwell at forty-two—and the oldest among them—Justice Young at sixty-five—are both originalists, but a twenty-three-year swing in age is significant. An age difference that spans six presidential elections is significant. I tend to favor putting young justices on a Court that needs long careers to establish long originalist legacies, and thus I would tend to favor the younger among them.

The state justices on the list of twenty-one could easily be part of the list of nominees to fill the thirteen vacancies in the federal circuit courts now pending. At the same time, there are thousands of qualified originalists for all of the 104 vacancies that exist on the federal bench as of this writing. There are other clues in the list: many have served not one but two clerkships for very reliable originalists like Justice Scalia himself, or Justice Clarence Thomas or Samuel Alito or Chief Justice Roberts—yes, he is a reliable originalist even if you disagree with his Obamacare decisions—and other luminaries of the originalist school like former federal judge J. Michael Luttig.

When President Obama set about to nominate a replacement for Justice Scalia I coined a hashtag—#NoHearingsNoVotes—that telegraphed a principled opposition to tipping the Supreme Court very hard to the left in an election year, an opposition that Senate

Majority Leader McConnell had already resolved upon. It was an opposition independent of the name and qualifications of whomever President Obama would eventually send to the Senate—it would turn out to be the very able jurist, but "living Constitution" enthusiast, Judge Merrick Garland—and that opposition to holding hearings and conducting votes would stick. Only one Republican senator broke with the Leader, Illinois's Mark Kirk, and he was defeated in November. The GOP caucus held firm and thus the Court was saved from a concrete block of five liberals.

There was a reason why Donald Trump's biggest applause line of his nomination acceptance speech in Cleveland was his recommitment to an originalist Supreme Court. "We are also going to appoint justices to the United States Supreme Court who will uphold our laws and our Constitution," then candidate Trump said, and this was met by a rising chorus of cheers and deafening applause.

Many conservatives uneasy with President Trump trusted him on this commitment and voted for him as a result. Why did we trust him on this? For me it was in part because I personally pressed him on it and on the appropriate response of the Senate should he depart from the commitment, in an interview on August 11, 2016:

Hugh Hewitt: Well, I've been writing about the Supreme Court a lot, and they keep telling me we can't trust Trump on his list of eleven, and I wrote hey, you don't have to trust Trump. If he departs from the list, I trust you, by the way, but if he departs, Mitch McConnell can block your nominee. First, can we trust you to live by that list? And second, if you didn't, would McConnell be justified in blocking your nominee?

Donald Trump: Yeah, number one, I'm going to live by that list or very close to it. It is possible there'll be somebody outside of that list that has very similar principles, and I think you don't want to totally preclude that. But the answer is yes, I'm living by the list, and yes, he can do whatever he wants, because it'll be either that list or somebody that is very close to it. In fact, I'm thinking about actually naming four or five more people to the list. You know, we had it vetted from the Federalist Society, and we had, and actually got the names from the Federalist, and that's considered pretty much the gold standard. We have Jim DeMint and his group . . .

HH: At Heritage, yeah.

Trump: . . . knows those names and respect those names. I have a lot of respect for Jim DeMint. And we have, you know, we have a great list. It's a great list of people. Yeah, I mean, if we veered from that, I would say block it, and I would be very happy with that. And I wouldn't even fight it, because I won't have to.

That's the lock, the guarantee: A GOP Senate that simply need not act on a name not on the list, an obstruction authorized in advance by the new president himself: "Yeah, I mean, if we veered from that, I would say block it, and I would be very happy with that. And I wouldn't even fight it, because I won't have to."

This says nothing about other vacancies that may arise on the Court—and I would not be surprised if Justice Anthony Kennedy retired this summer, secure in the irreversibility of *Obergefell v. Hodges* (for reasons discussed below) but concerned with whether he could extend his often brilliant federalism jurisprudence under a new majority. There might be other vacancies as well if, say, the always strategic Justice Clarence Thomas decides to enjoy retirement for a couple of decades and also allow a President Trump who has shown reliability on appointments to make way for a younger originalist. The Supreme Court might become a bastion—and not just an occasionally lighthouse of originalism—under the shrewd and playing-for-Marshall status guidance of the chief justice and the razor-sharp intellect of Justice Alito buttressed by Justice Thomas and one, two, or more young allies.

I wrote above that Justice Kennedy can be assured of the durability of *Obergefell.* I believe that in part because of the deeply embedded idea of "reliance" that runs through and binds tight the common law we inherited from England with the Constitution's own structure and the Court's long-standing understanding of the importance of stare decisis.

This concept is central to the stable, enduring "rule of law." *Stare decisis* means to abide by, or adhere to, decided cases, a bedrock principle in American law. Thus when the Supreme Court has once laid down a principle of law as applicable to a certain state of facts, it will adhere to that principle and apply it to all future cases where the facts are substantially the same and regardless of whether the parties and property are the same. It means, in laymen's terms, "been there, done that," and that the courts are sticking with their past decisions—most of the time. But not always.

Stare decisis is not an absolute principle. I noted above that the Court had to reverse the horrible decision of *Plessy v. Ferguson* from 1896, which upheld the evil charade of "separate but equal," and it took fifty-eight years to do so. Similarly, the First Amendment was scarred by previous decisions in two cases: *Austin v. Michigan Chamber of Commerce* in 1990 and *McConnell v. Federal Election Commission* in 2003. The Supreme Court's decision in the 2008 decision of *Citizens United* overturned the twenty-eight-year-old holding in *Austin* and partially overturned the five-year-old decision in *McConnell.*

So, in keeping with the principle of stare decisis, the Supreme Court almost always adheres to and abides by the decisions it has already handed down . . . until it doesn't. Why ought fans of *Obergefell* not worry about its being reversed, but at the same time critics be confident that *Roe v. Wade* and the *Planned Parenthood v. Casey* decision, which remade Roe into a slightly more coherent but still awful ruling on abortion, would likely fall with a couple of appointments to the Court by Donald Trump? Why can foes of the already tottering regime of affirmative action in higher education expect to see it fall, but other Court watchers be comforted to know that precedents of church-state separation will hold along with the cases concerning the status of women?

The answer on what decisions are likely to be upheld, and others are not, can be found in the concurring opinion of Chief Justice Roberts in *Citizens United* and in the concept of "reliance." I had to persuade my very expert editor to leave these paragraphs intact here, because while his language is a bit dense for a nonlawyer, it matters in countering the ridiculous notion that an originalist Court is an "activist" Court when in fact it is simply a Court for which the Constitution is a reliable and somewhat obvious guide. When you read through this, understand that the names of the cases referenced by the chief justice have been removed to make the meaning a bit more accessible for the non-lawyer. Most of the cases cited by the chief justice were famous—famously bad decisions that had to be overturned despite stare decisis acting as a general brake on throwing out old decisions.

So pardon the legalese but these six paragraphs from

the chief justice's concurrence in *Citizens United* matter a great deal in understanding what's ahead under a revitalized Supreme Court majority in favor of originalism but pledged as well to the general principle of stare decisis. If a reliable originalist five-member majority emerges, a bunch of bad decisions will be overturned but many that conservatives intensely dislike, such as *Obergefell,* won't. The chief justice's revealing opinion came in the context of him joining the majority in rejecting the previous decisions to allow corporations to spend without restriction during an election. He wanted to explain that this wasn't just throwing darts and legislating from the highest bench but was instead the application of both principles of fidelity to the original design (and limits) of the Constitution and the correct application of the principle of stare decisis. Stare decisis does not exist to protect bad decisions, he argued, especially when those decisions are harming the development of the law and the preservation of liberty. His second, less obvious point is that all nine of the justices have acted against stare decisis and joined majorities to overturn prior bad decisions. No one actually disagrees—on the Court or off—that bad decisions need to be overturned. Stare decisis counsels that the Court move very slowly to upend previous decisions, not that it never do so—and everyone knows this who cares to argue honestly about what the Court is doing on any given day. The originalists are going to try to overturn bad decisions only when the cost of doing so in terms of lost stability is less than the advantage of preserving liberty or the rule of law. Thus did *Brown v. Board* rightly strike down the terrible "separate can be equal" decision in *Plessy v. Ferguson*.

Roberts argues that fidelity to precedent—the policy of stare decisis—is vital to the proper exercise of the judicial function. He writes:

> "Stare decisis is the preferred course because it promotes the evenhanded, predictable, and consistent development of legal principles, fosters reliance on judicial decisions, and contributes to the actual and perceived integrity of the judicial process." . . . For these reasons, we have long recognized that departures from precedent are inappropriate in the absence of a "special justification." . . .
>
> At the same time, stare decisis is neither an "inexorable command". . . nor "a mechanical formula of adherence to the latest decision," especially in constitutional cases. If it were, segregation would be legal, minimum wage laws would be unconstitutional, and the Government could wiretap ordinary criminal suspects without first obtaining warrants. . . . As the dissent properly notes, none of us has viewed stare decisis in such absolute terms.
>
> Stare decisis is instead a "principle of policy." When considering whether to reexamine a prior

erroneous holding, we must balance the importance of having constitutional questions decided against the importance of having them decided right. As Justice Jackson explained, this requires a "sober appraisal of the disadvantages of the innovation as well as those of the questioned case, a weighing of practical effects of one against the other."

In conducting this balancing, we must keep in mind that stare decisis is not an end in itself. It is instead "the means by which we ensure that the law will not merely change erratically, but will develop in a principled and intelligible fashion." Its greatest purpose is to serve a constitutional ideal—the rule of law. It follows that in the unusual circumstance when fidelity to any particular precedent does more to damage to this constitutional ideal than to advance it, we must be more willing to depart from that precedent.

Thus, for example, if the precedent under consideration itself departed from the Court's jurisprudence, returning to the " 'intrinsically sounder' doctrine established in prior cases" may "better serv[e] the values of stare decisis than would following [the] more recently decided case inconsistent with the decisions that came before it." Abrogating the errant precedent, rather than reaffirming or extending it, might better preserve the

> law's coherence and curtail the precedent's disruptive effects.
>
> Likewise, if adherence to a precedent actually impedes the stable and orderly adjudication of future cases, its stare decisis effect is also diminished. This can happen in a number of circumstances, such as when the precedent's validity is so hotly contested that it cannot reliably function as a basis for decision in future cases, when its rationale threatens to upend our settled jurisprudence in related areas of law, and when the precedent's underlying reasoning has become so discredited that the Court cannot keep the precedent alive without jury-rigging new and different justifications to shore up the original mistake.

Here is everything a proponent of same-sex marriage needs to be reassured that the new Supreme Court will not disturb *Obergefell.* None of the reasons for reversing precedent and abandoning stare decisis laid out by the chief justice apply to that case. At the same time, the need for stability in the arrangements made by same-sex couples and their children—the reliance they have placed on the Court's sweeping decision in *Obergefell*—argue strongly for leaving the decision and Kennedy's jurisprudence in same-sex intimacy intact. By contrast, the Court and the country's ongoing abortion battles argue for the Court to withdraw from the field it ought never to have entered and leave the matter to the states to decide. Also, by very sharp contrast, the mess that the Court has made of the Religion Clauses must eventually be addressed and made right so that religious faith in all its forms is protected and not hounded from the public square or from private expression of any sort. The attempts to criminalize the exercise of conscience with fines and firings will have to be curbed by a Court animated by both the Declaration of Independence and by the Constitution, the two places where these rights of conscience were defined. It will be a hard task requiring deep thought and a special focus on explaining decisions to the public. The Court has done this before and it must do so again.

But it cannot sweep away what it has already done and pretend that it wasn't done when millions of Americans have come to understand that same-sex couples can marry anywhere and anytime and be subject to the same laws and rules concerning marriage as govern male-female marriage. Some conservatives and many people of faith will disagree with me on this, but I don't see how the Court can or should reverse the decision without enormous costs, and without any benefit that cannot otherwise be gained by a careful jurisprudence of religious liberty. The Court rushed in where many legislatures had gone or were headed, and where initiatives in states like California would surely have gone. The collective will of the large majority of Americans is now embodied in *Obergefell*. I do not see how any serious argument to overturn it will advance to a majority even of a Court eventually made up of nine judicial legatees of Justice Scalia.

"Reliance" means so much to the law. It is often the very first legal concept a first-year law student is introduced to, and it is the bedrock principle of "the rule of law." Everyone has to be able to rely on the laws as they are written and have been applied. Laws may change, but not retroactively, at least not in a just society. When you build your life on basic understandings of the rules as embodied in the Constitution, the sudden change in those rules causes enormous hardship and pain, as well as deep resentment in those who have relied on them.

The debate over same-sex marriage was so ferocious and its casualties so numerous that we need to collectively say "case closed."

This is of course not the case with the ongoing debates over abortion, which continue to rage forty years after *Roe v. Wade*, and will continue to do so as medical science and faith continue their collision with advocates of unlimited "reproductive rights." I do not see any instant and widespread effort to legislate around it as happened immediately after *Roe* and that continues to this year. Perhaps because abortion is believed by its opponents to concern the rights of unique humans who are not spoken for or defended in the womb, while marriage is a choice between two consenting people, the surrender by opponents of same-sex marriage is more complete than it ever was—or will be—on the issue of life.

In the meantime, the future jurisprudence of the Supreme Court will be what it will be on this and all other decisions, and I could be as wrong in this prediction as I was in most political predictions in 2016, but whatever the result of any future challenge to *Obergefell*, the president and his advisors need to move very quickly on the hundred or so other vacancies awaiting them (a number that grows and grows with each month). And here they could borrow with great advantage a concept from, of all places, the National Football League—specifically, the NFL Draft "war room" that exists inside the management offices of every one of the thirty-two NFL teams.

In each of those rooms, and in a thousand "virtual" war rooms that are the country's "mock draft" websites, people are making ongoing assessments of college football talent. The very best mockers are Dane Brugler, senior draft analyst for NFLDraftScout and for CBS Sports (follow this genius at @dpbrugler on Twitter); the superstars of draft day itself, Mel Kiper and Todd McShay of ESPN; WalterFootball; Matt Miller of Bleacher Report; and a dozen others. The list goes on and on—there is a "big board" on every site and in every NFL headquarters. This board ranks the very best players in the college game and continues down a list of five hundred or so NFL prospects. It is updated constantly and quarreled over in every room (and living room and bar) until the draft is over in April or May, and then it begins again immediately for the next season's draft. The careers of NFL executives and draft analysts depend on their ability to get these boards right.

Constant evaluation, constant ranking, constant input from hundreds of credible sources—that is the NFL Draft "process."

And thus it should be for President Trump's "war room" on judicial appointments. One board for the Supreme Court. One board for the U.S. circuit courts of appeals. One for the federal district courts. One for the specialized courts. If past is prologue, President Trump will make at least two hundred lifetime appointments to the federal courts, and each of those judges will render tens of thousands of rulings and hundreds of decisions that bind and guide the republic. The averages suggest federal judges are appointed in their early fifties and that they serve longer than twenty years. The trend seems to be that the judges begin serving at a younger age and serve longer. Whatever the average and whatever the trend, these judicial appointments are the bedrock of a president's long-term impact on the country.

The stakes surrounding these appointments go higher and higher. As the courts have expanded their reach, so has their collective importance to an individual president's legacy increased. Administrative agencies like the Environmental Protection Agency now regulate vast patches of industry on the stretched-beyond-recognition authority of the Clean Air Act—passed in 1963 and extensively amended in 1970, 1977, and 1990. The same goes for the United States Army Corps of Engineers using the Clean Water Act of 1972. It is also the case with the United States Fish and Wildlife Service using the Endangered Species Act of 1973. Disputes over the aggressive use of old laws in new contexts for new purposes land in the courts and are decided by the judges sitting there. Thus the importance of every single appointment to the federal bench has skyrocketed, so much of American life do these judges control and so vast are the changes they can command or put in motion. It takes decades to assess any particular appointment and even longer to render conclusions on a president's complete impact on the law, but it is beyond dispute that with these appointments the president lays the foundation of a lot of his legacy. So it has been with all previous modern presidents. So it will be with President Trump.

Thus the people to whom President Trump delegates the ranking of potential appointees will be among his most important counselors. If they are themselves "originalists," they will be assembling a "big board" of judicial candidates of extraordinary ability and willingness to serve as long as they can, faithful to the principles that brought them into consideration in the first place. Some judges "evolve" on the bench from "originalists" to "living Constitution" enthusiasts. A handful deceive their betters from the beginning. The former are to be sought after and promoted, the latter weeded out.

If President Trump is well served by his counselors, his mark on the courts will be enormous. And in making that mark he will be assisted every day by the unlikeliest of allies, former Senate majority leader Harry Reid.

Until Reid came along, it had required sixty votes to move a nominee to a vote and then to confirmation. But Reid orchestrated the unleashing of the "nuclear option" in November 2013. He changed the Senate rules so that the U.S. Senate can override a rule or precedent by a simple majority of 51 votes, instead of by a supermajority of 60 votes. The result: the 60-vote rule was gone in a day.

Paul Kane of the *Washington Post* summed it up well at the time. He wrote: "In the long term, the rule change represents a substantial power shift in a chamber that for more than two centuries has prided itself on affording more rights to the minority party than any other legislative body in the world. Now, a president whose party holds the majority in the Senate is virtually assured of having his nominees approved, with far less opportunity for political obstruction."

Kane and everyone else at the time recognized the change for what it was: "a substantial power shift in a chamber." Trying to redefine the Reid Rule now that the Democrats are in the minority and facing that status for what could be a very long run of years and a huge pile of nominees is already a cottage industry on the left. The Democrats made a big bet. They lost. They have to pay it off and the vigorish as well. Harry Reid and now Senate Minority Leader Chuck Schumer thought that the prospect of a Republican president and a Republican majority was a long way off, and that in the long run they would fare better by jamming through their nominees. How very, very wrong they were.

The "long term" turned out to have been less than four years away, for President Trump now has before him an open road to remake the federal judiciary. Where nominees once took 60 votes to confirm, they now only require 51. Where once genuine originalists had to almost be smuggled onto the bench, now they can be put forward proudly (and indeed defiantly, given prevailing supermajoritarian opinion in the nation's elite and elitist law schools, where "living Constitution" enthusiasts hold supermajority status on faculties, and indeed where many faculties cannot point to even a single originalist in their Constitutional law–teaching ranks). There is a panic in the law school faculty meetings now, but very few if any of the "progressives" in legal academia stepped forward to argue against Reid's trashing of the old filibuster rules when they thought it useful to their project of increasing the power and authority of the unelected judges drawn in large part, if not from their ranks, then at least from their universe of beliefs.

To repeat, again for emphasis because this matters so much and will matter even more in the years ahead: Reid and his colleagues tried to use pure sophistry at the time to limit the precedent they were establishing in 2013, saying it applied only to confirmations other than those to the Supreme Court. This is nonsense on stilts, of course—threadbare rhetoric used to try to conceal the actual fact of what was done: a change to the rules of the Senate by a simple majority of senators, not the 66 previously required to change the rules (and when the rule on filibusters had been lowered to 60, it took 66 votes to accomplish that). Once used, a maneuver that changes how the rules are changed changes those rules forever.

Read that again, slowly, for it matters a great deal: Once used, a maneuver that changes how the rules are changed changes those rules forever.

The precedent of simple majority confirmation of nominees is now the one and only rule of the Senate, the binding precedent, and will be used by either party whenever and for whomever that majority party wants in any position. Indeed, it can be used to break the rules governing legislative filibusters. The recklessness of Reid had no boundary and the unified GOP knows it cannot risk indulging their Democratic colleagues' feverish attempts to change history without a stunning rebuke from its own base. It may be that Senate traditionalists try to preserve the legislative filibuster, but not for appointments, and indeed there is no logic to preserving the legislative filibuster even given the crashing of the gates of the rules, but especially not for Supreme Court nominees who upset liberals and progressives because those nominees are originalists.

This shattering of precedent had its roots in campaigns to block nominees led by Reid and Senator Patrick Leahy of Vermont when George W. Bush was sending his candidates to the Senate. It was then GOP Senate Majority Leader Bill Frist who first threatened to use the nuclear option maneuver when Reid and Leahy turned aside vote after vote on extremely well-qualified nominees (including then private citizen John Roberts, denied a seat on the District of Columbia Circuit Court of Appeals under the first President Bush and again for a time under the second President Bush). Just before Frist detonated the nuclear option, the "Gang of Fourteen"—seven Democrats and seven Republicans—assembled in 2005 to do a deal that granted passage to many, but not all, of W's blockaded nominees. Frist did not have to trigger the nuclear option. Reid charged ahead eight years later, though, and broken is broken.

That means it would take every Democrat and at least three Republican senators to vote no to block a judicial nominee (or any executive branch nominee) in the years ahead. That may happen. But much more likely is the nomination and confirmation of scores of superbly qualified originalists who would never have passed the 60-vote hurdle, judges-in-waiting like Dr. John Eastman, my staunchly originalist colleague at the Fowler School of Law at Chapman University, former dean of that law school and clerk for Justice Thomas. I believe Dr. Eastman should be headed to the Tenth Circuit Court of Appeals, and that the executive director of the Yankee Institute and former *Harvard Law Review* managing editor Carol Platt Liebau would be a champion of freedom on the Second Circuit. Both should be atop the "big boards" for those circuits.

Before the Reid Rule blew up the 60-vote requirement, Republican presidents fretted too much about whether judges were "confirmable," and only rarely would they raise the "originalist" flag high and sail into battle. Now it is full Nelson all the time—"No captain can do very wrong if he places his ship alongside that of the enemy."

It may be that after at least three years of simple majority confirmations, Reid's replacement, the much more able Schumer, would try to sit down with Leader McConnell and adopt a new set of "old" rules for the Senate. That would mean three years of the Reid Rule's use by Republicans—the same amount of time that Harry Reid intended to use those rules for himself and President Obama (before he and the president "led" the Senate Democrats to a crushing, majority-losing defeat in November 2014), but there ought to be a debate about that far beyond the Senate chambers. The Framers did not include a filibuster in their design. They explicitly provided for a supermajority when it came to ratification of treaties (Article II, Section 2) and could easily have done so for judicial nominations had they thought it a necessary safeguard, but they did not. Thus the filibuster has always been, at best, extra-constitutional.

Ultimately Article I, Section 5 of the Constitution is the authority here: "Each House may determine the Rules of its Proceedings." The Senate cannot unilaterally change the number of votes required to ratify a treaty, nor can it decrease the number of senators necessary to convict a president of an impeachable offense as provided in Article I, Section 3: "The Senate shall have the sole Power to try all Impeachments. When sitting for that Purpose, they shall be on Oath or Affirmation. When the President of the United States is tried, the Chief Justice shall preside: And no Person shall be convicted without the Concurrence of two thirds of the Members present."

On everything not explicitly qualified, a majority of the Senate dictates the rules of the Senate. Harry Reid blew a hole in the Senate's precedents, and through that vast breach should now flow a continuous file of tested and true originalists. President Obama successfully nominated 329 federal judges, including 55 circuit court judges and 2 Supreme Court justices. President George W. Bush successfully nominated 327 federal judges, including 62 circuit court judges and 2 Supreme Court justices. Thanks to the Reid Rule, President Trump should be able to confirm more than half his predecessors' numbers in a single term, to every level. Thanks, Harry Reid. Thanks very, very much.

They should be on the lookout especially for nominees committed to an expansive vision of the Free Exercise Clause of the First Amendment, for it is concern over imperiled religious freedoms that animated much of the Donald Trump vote, from evangelicals to Mass-attending Catholics.

Let's begin with the enlargement of the United States Court of Appeals for the District of Columbia Circuit.

Harry Reid actually broke the filibuster in order to "pack" the D.C. Circuit, widely regarded as the second most important court because of its supervisory role over the enormous federal bureaucracy. By loading up the D.C. Circuit with "progressives," President Obama and Harry Reid guaranteed a home-field advantage for the president's bureaucrats' far-reaching rules. Again, turnabout is fair play in politics. Balance should be restored to the D.C. Circuit through the addition of three new judgeships, and those judgeships should be filled with originalists keen to curb the otherwise nearly ungovernable administrative state. If the new, unified GOP government is genuinely committed to rolling back the federal government to its Constitutional banks, TPRM will address this quickly and move to lower the judicial barricade that rollback will have to cross in the form of the "packed" D.C. Circuit.

Some old-school Republicans groused about the size of the D.C. Circuit for years, grumbling it was too large for its workload. (Some used that argument as an excuse for inaction on President Obama's activist nominees, a transparent dodge for some who would have been better served, and who would have served better, had they simply and straightforwardly said, "No, not that nominee for this court. Not now, not in an era of a president with no respect for the rule of law.")

Senators serious about restoring the Constitution to its rightful place will expand the D.C. Circuit as an urgent, first-hundred-days priority. It's an obscure issue but a key one to winning the future for limited government.

Also obscure, but also less urgent and important, is breaking up the behemoth Ninth Circuit. Right now the Ninth Circuit includes nine states and two territories—15 separate "judicial districts,"—and has 29 "active" circuit judges and 19 "senior status" circuit judges (semi-retired judges who sit on cases). The circuit is lopsidedly left-wing, and many of the states governed by these 29 judges are conservative. And Judge Stephen Reinhardt is the poster child for a liberal judge and he is often reversed on obvious grounds by the Supreme Court.

Breaking up the Ninth Circuit into two or three circuits would serve federalist interests very well by giving the West Coast and Hawaii a circuit every bit as liberal as its voters and elected officials, and yet also allowing the mountain west and the desert states judicial representation far more in keeping with their cultures and politics. Federalism is poorly suited by a one-left-wing-size-fits-all Ninth Circuit. Again, narrow-bore conservatives worried about the costs of a few courthouses and judicial salaries are wildly indifferent to the wrongs done to the Constitution by the current arrangement.

The third priority applies to every federal judge at every level. Each would-be nominee ought to be obliged to read Lynne Cheney's magisterial biography, *James Madison: A Life Reconsidered,* before interviewing for the judgeship they desire, and to be prepared to discuss the controversies giving rise to the First Amendment's religion clauses and to the Virginia Statute for Religious Freedom before them. The Framers did not intend to ever encourage, much less tolerate, the hostility to faith that now pervades the public square, and indeed would be sickened by it, even those who could in no way be described as devout Christians. "They knew liberty," as I told Justice Breyer, and they would never have countenanced a jurisprudence that obliges people of faith to bend the knee before the secular absolutism that is rising in America. That a photographer with religious objections to using his or her art to memorialize a same-sex wedding could be penalized for the refusal, or a pharmacist could lose his or her license for a refusal to dispense abortifacients—these events would shock them as they shock most modern Americans who understand intuitively and comprehensively where the border exists between an unlawful and unwanted "establishment of religion" and its robust free exercise. Trying to use Obamacare to make the Little Sisters of the Poor accessories to abortion was always repugnant to the vast majority of Americans, but so too was the shuttering of adoption services by Boston Catholic Charities in 2006 when facing a mandate to assist in adoptions for same-sex couples on the same basis as heterosexual married couples. How could "progressives" place religious freedom behind support for same-sex marriage when they knew—they knew—that the millennia-old Catechism of the Roman Catholic Church could not change simply because the opinions on marriage of the Massachusetts Supreme Judicial Court had changed?

I do not believe *Obergefell* will be overturned, but I do believe, hope, and pray that a Free Exercise Clause equal to the task set out for it by the Framers will reappear and will overprotect rather than underprotect religious liberty. It was for religious liberty that the country was founded in large part. If the election of 2016 keeps secure that liberty and with it the ability of American Christians to evangelize the world, the explanation of why evangelicals and Mass-attending Catholics supported Donald Trump will be self-evident. Belief in the dignity of all people—gay or straight, faith-filled or as nonbelieving as Richard Dawkins—needs to reanimate our Supreme Court decisions, and a genuine protection for a life lived in conformity to conscience must reappear as vibrant as it ever was, as complete as it was imagined by Jefferson and Madison.

A final note on courts, and one perhaps unexpected but vital to the successful renewal of the American federal judiciary. Federal judges are woefully underpaid. Their counterparts in private practice make seven-figure salaries—as these judges could if they leave the bench. Too many great judges have retired as they contemplated college costs for their children. Spare me lectures on public service. I'm not suggesting they be paid millions. But salaries of a half million annually are reasonable. Yes, they are. And the additional cost of that measure is nothing compared to the cost of having originalist judges leave and bureaucracies run unchecked over the rights of all Americans. Raise the salaries of judges in the first hundred days. The return on investment will be huge.

V

The Free Market Flourishing

There's a Fourth Way on tax and entitlement reform. I'm not a "tax reform" guy. Never have been. Never will be. I know it floats a lot of people's boats, that endless discussions roll on and on about marginal tax rates, and that Grover Norquist has spent decades collecting cards with signatures on them committing the signers to never vote to raise tax rates. The federal tax scheme was overhauled pretty well by Ronald Reagan thirty years ago and it really isn't that bad, except for the corporate tax rate, which is insane, and the death tax, which is immoral. Specifically, the death tax is immoral when applied to financial legacies of less than $100 million dollars.

On the subject of tax reform, I sought out the views of my trusted friend Hank Adler. Hank and I wrote the book *The FairTax Fantasy*. Hank was a tax partner at Deloitte & Touche until he retired in 2003, and has been teaching accounting to college kids since then for fun. (Don't ask me to explain that. Like tax lawyers, tax accountants enjoy their work.) He's a public-spirited man and a savvy board member of big concerns. He has spent his life working through the consequences of various "tax reforms" and "tax cuts." He's very practical.

I want to begin this chapter with an appeal to the tax wonks of D.C.: get your heads out of the editorial pages of the *Wall Street Journal,* please! Real people don't live there. They live in high-tax states, in three-bedroom homes that are the centerpiece of their families' lives. They go to churches that they support with tax-deductible contributions. They live in communities anchored by institutions like hospitals and colleges that depend on very large tax-deductible contributions. The purists at the *Wall Street Journal* want to end all deductions. They want a flat rate, and they are steeped in a world of efficiency and non-distorted economic decision-making, whereas most Americans live in houses they love surrounded by families they'd like to see prosper.

Most tax theorists, but especially the purists of the "Austrian school," wouldn't mind condemning most Americans to a life of economic upheaval if they could just have their way on crazy ideas like eliminating the mortgage interest deduction. I understand they read books by Austrian economists and attend seminars where everyone nods in agreement about the need for ending market distortions. But politics says they are nuts.

People like their homes. They bought them on the promise of the mortgage interest rate deduction and they made life decisions to stay in high-tax states based on the deductibility from adjusted gross income on federal tax returns of state income taxes. They give to their churches, the Salvation Army, Catholic Charities, United Way, and the Injured Marine Semper Fi Fund in part because the donations are tax-deductible. Mess with the tax code because you are in love with theory and you end up with a political wipeout.

President Trump understands this because, once upon a time, he and his father built housing for people in the middle class. They know what owning a home means to people. Reducing or eliminating the home mortgage deduction will revalue every house in America. That's how housing markets work. My pal the economist Richard McKenzie estimates it's a minimum 10 percent hit on the felt value of personal wealth if the anti-deduction enthusiasts have their way. Try selling that in 2018. Or the unintended consequences of devaluing the national market by at least 10 percent or more overnight.

"Capping" the mortgage interest deduction has exactly the same effect on the overall market since it will devalue the value of the highest-valued house, causing the trickle-down devaluation to spread out as the first consequence of Trump tax policy. Thus I was shocked to hear in the very first statement of Steven Mnuchin, in his first interview on CNBC's *Squawk Box* after his selection for secretary of the Treasury by then President-elect Trump on November 30, 2016, that the mortgage interest deduction would be capped in a Trump tax reform. Mnuchin and Wilbur Ross, Trump's pick for commerce secretary, had been talking about 4 percent growth, about cutting the corporate tax rate, about "a big tax cut for the middle class," and then threw off that the administration would "cap mortgage interest but allow some deductibility." Presto, Team Trump went to war with every homeowner in America not because of the deduction but because of the value of their homes, and started, almost casually, a shooting war with the National Association of Realtors (NAR). "The mortgage interest deduction (MID) is a remarkably effective tool that facilitates home ownership," the NAR bluntly declares on its website. "NAR opposes any changes that would limit or undermine current law." The NAR had 1,241,548 members on the day Secretary Mnuchin made that casual announcement, and that day they began to dislike Donald Trump, to become enemies of his Congressional majorities, to become enemies of his reelection, because suddenly his chief economic advisor was threatening their jobs, their livelihoods, and their families. And as this army of very skilled communicators begins to explain what "capping" does to the value of every home in America—every home, it is all one market—the army of opposition and anger grows, and it is directed at President Trump.

This deduction, which survived the great reform of 1986, did so because it is so politically potent and economically charged. Wealthy people have never understood this, or the impact of dumping the state income tax deduction (which would put newly red states like

Pennsylvania, Michigan, Ohio, North Carolina, and Wisconsin, with state income tax rates of 3 percent, 4.25 percent, 4.997 percent, 5.75 percent, and 7.65 percent, respectively, back on the table for Democrats within six months after flipping them—and for what, to win the no-state-income-tax states of Florida and Texas twice?)

The theorists tell us we will all do better, but the practical impact of just these two changes is devastating to middle- and upper-middle-class voters. It's nuts, and beyond nuts, it wreaks havoc again on promises people were made by the federal government about where they could live and what it would cost, promises that are baked into every economic cake of every family, promises on which voters have relied. Want to destroy the remaining few congressional Republicans in California? Or New York? Or the more numerous but facing-redistricting-soon Republicans in the blue-turned-red states? Turn average taxpayers against you by devaluing their home just as home prices have returned to where they were before the Great Recession and taking deductions off their taxes. They won't believe they are getting tax relief. They won't. That's why these deductions survive. Repealing or "capping" them to appeal to the purists, to the *Wall Street Journal* Republicans, but not to President Trump's new Republicans and not to many of the millions of old-school Republicans as well.

People like their churches, their colleges, and their charities of choice. Americans use charitable deductions to support their communities, and they rely on the big institutions that need big gifts to thrive. They don't mind buildings with names on them. It's how we get things built that don't look like Stalinist DMVs.

And just as they can't afford to tear up their lives and move from California and New York and other high-tax states because the *Wall Street Journal* Republicans want to remove the state income tax deduction, and they don't want the institutions they love—churches, colleges, hospitals—to fade or crumble because the big donations on which they depend have gone from tax-advantaged to nonexistent. Come down from the clouds and live in the world that reliance on the existing tax code created. "Hey, why should Texas subsidize California?" is glib, but Texans don't actually feel that way or vote for that reason. Understand that justice requires that no changes to basic pillars of American economic life be crafted in backrooms, that no pillars of real life for millions be pulled down in order to celebrate some sort of a Hayekian triumph of theory over practice. We don't need a *Lord of the Flies: The Economists' Edition.*

There's work to be done, certainly, and my "real-world" expert Hank Adler, who has spent a lifetime studying this, weighs in in Appendix D. The key is not marginal rates, but simplicity, certainty, steadiness, and a sense of justice. The reason the absurd "FairTax" got any traction at all was the appeal of its name, not its crazy, unworkable scheme. Whatever is done to the tax code has to be capable of explanation in short, concise fashion by the president and the Speaker and the Senate majority leader. If they propose to mess with people's lives, it had better be for a good reason and not that gross domestic product will rise in years four through six of some 4 percent GDP growth surge.

Entitlement reform: This is actually relatively easy by contrast with tax reform because (1) it can be explained, (2) it comports with a basic understanding of fairness, and (3) its economic impact should be quantified: "Folks, we live longer and want to live longer still, so we are moving the retirement age to 68, and in 10 years it is going to 70, and in 10 more to 72. We can reverse that if needed but our actuarial staff says that's the real deal. If you are over 55, no worries. If you are 54 or younger, plan accordingly. And, oh, by the way, nobody really understands this, but we are 'unchaining' the cost of living increase from the Consumer Price Index. You won't notice the few dollars a month less you won't be getting in ten years because—wait for it—it is ten years down the road! Don't believe the schemers and screamers from AARP. Thank you."

Gradualism on entitlement reform will work because it makes sense and does not threaten immediate upheaval. There is AARP, but there is also AMAC, a longtime sponsor of my radio show and a growing conservative membership association for seniors.

AARP will gag and scream, but so what? This entitlement reform stuff is uncontroversial outside the Beltway if the unified GOP government keeps its delayed impact to those under the age of fifty-five. Medicare changes will be more controversial but still doable if reformers tell patients the real deal. The 2015 Medicare Access and CHIP Reauthorization Act (MACRA) has begun to work reform already and more will follow under the leadership of new Health and Human Services secretary Dr. Tom Price. He's a gifted communicator, as is Speaker Ryan, on these issues. With partners in the Senate and the White House, any case for the reform of Medicare must be carefully and repeatedly made, and voters must be persuaded. This can be accomplished because Democrats have crashed their credibility. That cratering of credibility in the post-Obamacare meltdown creates a unique opportunity: an already defeated opponent. The unified GOP has to do something grand; there will be a lot of shouting. Do it fast. Stand up and defend it in 2018. Don't hang around halfway up the mountain, taking fire from above and below. Go Nike: just do it.

And fix Social Security disability, which *Forbes* branded a "200 Billion-a-Year 'Disability-Industrial Complex,'" built around what NPR's Chana Joffe-Walt described as a skyrocketing rise of disability in America. "Every month," Joffe-Walt reported, "14 million people get a disability check from the government." That's up from 7.2 million recipients of the federal benefits who were receiving them in 2002—just fifteen years ago.

"There's no diagnosis called disability," Joffe-Walt

continued. "You don't go to the doctor and the doctor says, 'We've run the tests and it looks like you have disability.' It's squishy enough that you can end up with one person with high blood pressure who is labeled disabled and another who is not."

The "trust fund" that receives the payments workers make and pays out the disability benefits that are claimed and awarded will be broke at the end of 2023, because right now every dollar in benefits paid is only being replaced with 80 cents in payroll tax contributions. The average disabled worker's benefit is $1,166, but with so many millions receiving it every month, the escalating costs have bankrupted the program. The reporting suggests that a cottage industry of lawyers and counselors has figured out how to game the system into paying benefits to many millions of people who are not what most taxpayers would think of as disabled. The subject is dense and dull and deeply upsetting to those who every day go to work with discomfort or severe pain. What is going to make everyone mad is that in six to seven years the benefits will have to be cut even to the deeply and genuinely, beyond-any-doubt disabled Americans. That's the consequence of unreformed entitlements. Bankruptcy and benefit cuts to people who deeply and genuinely need or have earned benefits.

Supplemental Security Income (SSI) shouldn't be a lottery for an early retirement but it does need to save those who are ravaged by bad luck and worse genes.

This is best done in one big bill. All will be well if it is wrapped into an immigration overhaul.

Even Medicaid can be fixed and the Obamacare fiasco repaired if the GOP resolves to take bad press from the left in return for positive reform for all. Medicaid, which covers the poorest Americans, cost about $545 billion last year. Seventy-two million out of 323 million Americans are on this subpar insurance. The program expanded under Obamacare, but the quality and quantity of health care for the poor did not. Low-wage citizens are getting less health care than the middle class and are getting way too much of it through emergency rooms.

On June 22, 2016, House Republicans released the "Health Care" component of the caucus's "A Better Way" policy proposals, which framed the election for House members seeking reelection. It is easily found by googling "A Better Way" and "Health Care." I covered its release on the radio show but in the trench warfare of the long and brutal presidential campaign it was lost, one more failed offensive against the near-continuous coverage of Clinton-Trump.

One thing is easily recalled, though: the House GOP repeated its calls for a block grant of Medicaid moneys to the states, first called for in 1981 by President Reagan and recommended repeatedly by President Bush. The theory is straightforward: Here's your federal check, states. Find a way to get health care to the poorest residents in your state. It's a capped budget, not an open-ended entitlement. It will be a radical step forward and one roundly denounced by the left, as will the repeal of Obamacare. But the health care system is in crisis, and the left's turn at the plate was the biggest legislative whiff in modern memory, a catastrophe for millions and an expensive misery for tens of millions. Only the wealthy face medical emergencies and complex diseases without financial pain. Every day Secretary Price and Speaker Ryan are going to have to take a stand and explain how Social Security Disability Insurance (SSDI), Medicare, Medicaid, and Obamacare are all parts of one problem. It is a problem that requires extensive surgeries just as the physical reconstruction of a shattered body does. Recovery is possible, but not until the surgeries are complete. Everyone cares about health care. Even the fittest triathletes care and know eventually they will need the health care system to be there for them. And everyone—everyone—knows it is terribly broken.

Compared to health care reform, tax reform is sleep inducing. Do you know one person who has woken up at 3 a.m. worrying about the national debt? Yes, it is an enormous problem and yes, it needs a thirty-year fix, but leading with it means leading with your political chin. Mix tax and entitlement reform with infrastructure investments and an immigration overhaul, and the voters who sent Donald Trump to Washington will nod and say, "Yes, yes, good for them. The GOP is getting everything done, quickly, and rightly so." Stand any part up alone and head back to the minority in 2018. It is that simple.

How do I know this? Because I talk to people. Hundreds of thousands of people every day, and they talk, on air and off. Elected officials do a lot of talking but not a lot of listening. They hear the distress of the victims of Obamacare but they really do not have a national view, not even senators. Especially on tax and entitlement reform.

I claim some special expertise because I have been down the road of warning about political consequences. In December 2013, then House budget chair Paul Ryan and Senator Patty Murray (D-WA) worked out for their respective majorities in the House and Senate a "budget deal." Part of that deal was a tiny bit of entitlement reform—a cut to the promised retirement benefits of active-duty and retired military, benefits that had been earned in uniform for service going back decades. I was first astonished, then appalled, then outraged. Not-yet Speaker Ryan came on my show a month after the deal was signed amid rising blowback and attempted to defend the deal he had struck. We agreed to disagree and because of his commitment to persuasion he has returned to the show, but that day there were sparks. Big sparks. It wasn't fair to begin entitlement reform with immediate benefit cuts—not benefit cuts limited to just new enlistees and new officers but also to already retired and active-duty career military who had relied on promises made when they made career decisions and reenlistment decisions. I understood that and heard hundreds of outraged callers agree with me. Ryan did his best to stop the GOP caucus from bolting on him but it did: the fallout from the military and their families and those who admire their service overwhelmed every argument he and his colleagues made. The "reform" was repealed. It was not fair, and it appeared out of nowhere—a standalone, one-off bout of entitlement reform that targeted the military. That won't fly.

When the dust settled I continued to ask myself how a brilliant legislator like Paul Ryan could get something so obvious so wrong. The Speaker is a strong supporter of the military. He was not insincere in his arguments. He just underestimated the political blowback that arrives when fairness is breached. How could that happen?

The same way a run at the home mortgage interest rate deduction comes about, or any of a dozen other major political missteps of the postwar era: the Bubble.

Good and well-meaning people in Washington, D.C., think about government all day, every day. It is their calling and joy. Even though they may complain about its foibles they wouldn't live anywhere else or do anything else. Hill staff, career bureaucrats, elected and appointed officials, everyone from the new president down to the summer intern at a new, poorly funded think tank love being where the world is actually governed. I joke that D.C. is the new Rome, meaning as in the old Roman

Empire, and it really is. It is certainly as wealthy. There is nothing like the vast collections of wealth of Silicon Valley's new tycoons or the concentrated attention on moneymaking of Manhattan or the odd and complex finance of Hollywood, with its added element of glamour. Washington, D.C., is simply where the power is, and the power talks to the power and enjoys doing so. The "inner ring" is much at work here. There are the three branches and a fourth estate; a Pentagon and K Street, the think tanks, and a thousand "associations" representing hundreds of thousands of businesses. There are hierarchies within hierarchies, socialites, news stars, and committee chairmen, fundraising captains and intense experts and authorities of very small but very important fiefdoms.

And they all talk to each other, and only the electeds get out very much to the country. So when the electeds get told something from the permanent class it is likely to have been shaped by assumptions long shared by that class, whether it is of the left or of the right, the R permanent class or the D permanent class.

I left in 1989 and did not come back, except for occasional visits, until 2016. I had forgotten the intense pull of the place toward a sense of authority mixed with superiority, and an internal ranking of power as subtle as the Pentagon's is structured, with its ranks and lines of command. The city swelled in the Obama years, growing more wealthy and powerful as federal spending skyrocketed and federal power soared. Again, the Beltway is not a few thousand people with huge fortunes like in Manhattan and Silicon Valley, but rather it is tens of thousands of folks of very upper-middle-class and very low-upper-class means and actual real power over other citizens' lives—people like the IRS's Lois Lerner, people who believe, genuinely, that they "know better."

And in fact they do know better—about some things. I don't know how to run the Export-Import Bank; I just know that we need one. I can't run, say, the Marine Corps Logistics Command or even OPM's Federal Health Benefits Program. (Anymore—I used to run the last thing in the last years of Reagan, an unbelievably large job to give to a thirty-two-year-old lawyer but someone had to do it. That happens a lot here.)

This isn't a book about the culture of D.C., though surely there is another Samuel Pepys, the famous British parliamentarian/diarist at work on as massive a scale. But the point for our purposes is that the vast juggernaut of authorities comes to a conclusion via its own ways and it is hard to shake it of that conclusion. One of those conclusions—which I shared—was that President Donald Trump could not win because he is so unlike everything else in Washington, D.C.; and not just now, but ever! The tone-deafness about active-duty military and retiree benefits was a tiny glimpse of just how insulated D.C. is from the rest of America. D.C.'s culture promotes the terrible conviction that "we know better."

And of course they don't. They can't. They can know,

for example, the intricacies of SSDI far better than me, or the difficulties of moving Medicaid in block grants to the state. Some will know the ins and outs of the home mortgage deduction far better than me. But I know my audience, and my audience—though this is not believed by the left—is Americans who watch D.C. with a keen, sharp interest. And that audience talks to me. And I listen to it. It is an ongoing and constructive dialogue. It does not tell me crystal-ball things like who was going to win Michigan. Instead, it reveals to me levels of pain and discomfort, anxiety and joy, comfortability with the status quo and an intense desire for change. After 9/11 the desire to strike back was so palpable that I am amazed Washington did not invade Canada. I still marvel at the calming effect of George W. Bush after 9/11. In 2008 the fear of complete collapse was so profound that we do need to credit the personality of President Obama for calming down nerves. (And God bless him for being a wonderful husband and dad under pressure when there are so many husbands and dads under pressure who use the pressure as an excuse to crack on their families.)

There aren't any more bad people here than there are bad people everywhere else, and my faith tells me we're all pretty bad. But the particular sin of the place is pride, pride, pride. Hearing someone say "I don't know" is an uncommon and thrilling thing. I have gotten used to saying it after twenty-eight years on the air—it is an essential defense system, a key to surviving on-air, but it is an important ability that is way too rare in Washington, D.C.

Dr. Larry Arnn is the president of Hillsdale College, a very good friend, a wise man, a superb teacher, and famous among conservatives for wit and prudence. His institution is erupting with young scholars who rush to Washington (and to Hillsdale's Kirby Center) to be a part of it all. But Arnn stays put mostly in a small town in Michigan, studying the Framers, Lincoln, and Churchill. He comes on my show once a week and we talk about the old books and big ideas, and the audience loves it. (All those 200+ hours of listening on subjects that begin with Homer and are as recent as the election of President Trump are available for binge listening at HughforHillsdale.com.)

What Dr. Arnn likes to point out most often—and he likes to talk, a lot, and he likes to mock me, a lot, and it is good talking and very funny mocking—is that the people decide in this country, and they do it through a mechanism of "constitutional majorities" molded by a collection of geniuses, made better by a genius named Lincoln, defended by a genius named Churchill and artful colleagues like FDR and George Marshall and Ike and MacArthur when its entire being was threatened by Hitler and Japan, defended again and triumphant under Reagan and the first Bush (the latter saw the successful unraveling of the old enemy), stewarded well by W and now in part handed over to Donald Trump. Dr. Arnn is an optimist because the people spoke loud and clear through its "constitutional majority." (Arnn and serious people care not a lick about the popular vote because that is not how we have ever contested, much less won, the White House since the first presidential election that began on December 15, 1788, and wrapped up on January 10, 1789. We won't ever pick a president that way unless the republic falls due to some disaster).

Early in 2015, Arnn and I moved into "Switzerland on the radio" as we began talking about the large GOP field of would-be Republican nominees. We did so because we wanted to be fair and talk about it with the other candidates, and because he serves many parts of the conservative movement. I was very critical of Donald Trump when he attacked Judge Curiel. I thought he was endangering the entire conservative movement with ill-chosen words and an emotional attack that he didn't even understand sounded racist to its core. (And as I have said from the first day I interviewed him—which I've done fifteen times, as well as posed questions to him in four debates and talked privately with him—he is not a racist!) When the *Access Hollywood* video surfaced I urged him to withdraw because it was a shocking thing and I thought it doomed him and thus the Supreme Court. I thought if he withdrew Mike Pence had a clear path to victory. It did not doom Trump. Because of something Arnn said early and often over the past two years.

"Something fundamental is afoot," Dr. Arnn also said. "This election is really about whether the government shall govern the people or the people govern the government." High-sounding words, but true, and Arnn was right more often than anyone else about Donald Trump and his appeal—and Arnn does not live inside the Beltway and does not do much media. Instead, he reads history and thinks about it, reads the Framers and Lincoln and studies Churchill and statesmanship. So he had the key. He called the shot about as well as anyone: the people were furious with the arrogance, and they sent the loudest message that could be sent.

Because of this message I am urging clarity on the priorities and speed on the execution and to abandon all caution on entitlements. Go for it, TPRM; go for it and do it all. Make it a one hundred days dizzying in their speed and accomplishment, but don't do stupid things. Don't threaten people's hard-won homes, their families, their churches. And get government out of their lives.

Which brings me back to the tax code, and Hank Adler.

Adler has spent a career in the details of the tax code and his retirement teaching its intricacies to would-be accountants. I leave to him in Appendix D the 30,000-foot view of what real tax reform means. But I summarize his deeply thought through positions: It's the simplicity, stupid. Not the marginal rates. Not the deductions. The simplicity of execution. You can keep a handful of key deductions that benefit everyone owning a home or living in a high-tax state or giving to charity, and you can keep an enormously complex tax code, for the 5 percent of Americans who pay most of the income tax. But as Hank explains, it has to be made so that the IRS doesn't consume your life for weeks every year or that the fear of mistakes haunts honest folks.

From me there are three tax reform suggestions I hope Speaker Ryan and Ways and Means Chair Kevin Brady consider. Again, my advantage is talking to people. Three hours a day. Five days a week. Forty-eight weeks a year, all across the country. For seventeen years. All three are the commonsense suggestions of an outsider political analyst and constitutional law professor who has long lived outside the Beltway, and who has spoken with tens of thousands of callers and guests about taxes generally and their deep disgust with being "managed" on their economic decisions from D.C., a "management" in love with changing the rules every few years despite the freedom-loving voters' continued attempts to set and reset their lives according to D.C.'s dictates. The three suggestions take as a starting point two facts:

First, the Employee Benefit Research Institute (EBRI) concluded in May 2015 that 25.8 million individual retirement accounts (IRAs) existed in the United States, owned by 20.6 million unique individuals. Combined, these accounts contained $2.46 trillion worth of assets.

Second, a Bloomberg News review of the securities

filings of 304 corporations found that these U.S. companies held $2.10 trillion in profits overseas, untaxed by the American government, because of the absurdly high rate of corporate profits taxation here at home. "Eight of the biggest U.S. technology companies added a combined $69 billion to their stockpiled offshore profits over the past year," concluded Bloomberg's Richard Rubin, with "Microsoft Corp., Apple Inc., Google Inc. and five other tech firms now account[ing] for more than a fifth" of the cash stockpile. Rubin's article is from March 2015. The stockpile has soared since then.

So, to my suggestions.

Want a massive tax cut to juice everything? Allow Americans to withdraw 10 percent of their retirement savings tax-free and without penalty.

Want a very, very happy population of voters? Allow everyone to use up to half of their tax-protected savings to pay their home mortgages down or completely off, increasing their sense of economic security and freeing up their budgets from the strain of their mortgage payments. Not only would such a move vastly improve Americans' sense of economic security, it would establish a foundation for retirement and free their saving and spending habits to more than make up for the phantom "lost revenue" in the faraway years when their retirement withdrawals would have been taxed under the current system.

Naysayers argue this puts retirees at risk when in

fact it does nothing of the sort: It would vastly increase their sense of well-being and if the nanny state was really worried, it could provide that mortgages so reduced or paid off could not have the asset they have secured—the primary home of the taxpayer—sold before age eighty without a tax payment or penalty of the sort that attaches presently to early withdrawals.

Some stock market correction would occur because of withdrawn assets, yes, but money is flowing into the United States right now and never has there been a better chance to clear off debt and increase standards of living—using Americans' own money. The "tax cut" of the 10 percent withdrawal would at least in part go right back into securities anyway, or to long-needed repairs or debt reduction. Don't overthink it: let Americans use their own money as best they see fit, and take less of it at the start.

As for suggestion three, even Democrats pretty much recognize the need to quickly lower our corporate tax rate. But do it in two phases.

Create a six-month "repatriation window" for the $2 trillion in corporate profits stranded abroad. Tax the repatriations at, say, 15 percent before raising the general rate to 20 percent. (Or 10 and 15 percent—the point is to greatly advantage the rapid return of the profits stranded abroad.) Then use the flood of revenue—"incentives matter," as Dr. McKenzie likes to tell me, and the stranded profits will zip back and fast—to pay for the infrastructure programs and the defense rebuild. Perhaps $300 billion in new tax revenue wouldn't materialize in the next six months, but much of it would.

Beltway sharpies will have a lot of reasons to say these things won't work. Beltway sharpies would have had disdain for the Homestead Act of 1862 as well. But the elegance of simplicity does indeed work on tax policy. Get Americans some of their own money, let them pay off or pay down their home mortgage debt, and get the profits of American companies home (with a kicker—see below). Watch growth return at multiples of the Obama years.

Now that kicker. Here the Fourth Way does a short-term dance with industrial policy. If Apple and Microsoft and Google are going to bring home a windfall, President Trump's art of the deal ought to take center stage in conversations with them all, based on this simple fact: the boom of Ann Arbor.

My alma mater—the University of Michigan Law School—used to turn out the most valuable thing in the whole Wolverine State: a U of M law degree. It traveled. It brought employment. It brought near guarantees of economic success. That's why I, an Ohio lad through and through, treated Michigan like the early Vikings treated England—land there, grab what was worth grabbing, and get out. (Go Bucks! Twelve out of thirteen is a good beginning to an even-longer streak of Jim Tressel–Urban Meyer orchestrated domination.)

But there's a new asset in Ann Arbor, aside from its great university. It is the Google campus there. Google landed there ten years ago, a sharp move for a growing giant looking for smart people and affordable housing in a great center of culture and learning (if not college football—go Bucks!). In the late spring of 2015, Google announced a major expansion of their presence in Ann Arbor. A May 1, 2015, *Detroit Free Press* article by Nathan Bomey trumpeted that "[i]nternet giant Google is planning a major expansion of its Ann Arbor operation, with plans to construct a new facility near the University of Michigan's North Campus.

"The company confirmed that it will relocate its current operations out of downtown Ann Arbor to a new corporate campus on the city's north side," Bomey reported.

Now, flash forward seventeen months, to a November 9 article in the *Toronto Star* by Steve Friess on the commercial real estate boom and consequent shortage in Ann Arbor, because it has become a high-tech hub and start-up machine. "[T]he area suddenly took on a tech-hub vibe, whereas for decades it had primarily focused on serving the university community," Freiss wrote of the somewhat run-down downtown I recall so well from the early 1980s.

"Since [Google moved in], other startups and branches of tech companies have alighted in Ann Arbor's downtown core," Friess continued before noting the consequence: jobs, jobs, jobs. "More than 60 companies took part in a recent job fair put on by the city's small-business incubator, Spark," he noted as an obvious sign of the whirling economic activity in and around Ann Arbor.

What Google did for Ann Arbor, it—and Apple and Microsoft and Facebook, et al.—can do for Warren, Ohio; Dubuque, Iowa; Erie, Pennsylvania; Milwaukee, Wisconsin; and every other Rust Belt state left behind by globalization. Ann Arbor is not unique in having a major university campus that can attract a huge branch of a giant high-tech company. All the old industrial giants have a suitable nearby campus too. Youngstown-Warren can draw on a dozen schools within forty-five minutes' driving distance, and Youngstown State, at the center of the Mahoning Valley, is much like Wichita State, which industrialist and free-market prophet Charles Koch has long extolled as a geyser of hardworking, talented young employees. Having a U of M degree helps, but there are lots of U of Ms around, and crucially, the old Rust Belt has all the infrastructure of growth in place: roads, electricity, schools, and homes of all sizes and values because it once was (and perhaps will once again be) home to the industry of the country and the wealth that country created.

The old "blue wall" region also has weather, but growth is indifferent to cold or rain or snow, and even the occasional lake-effect-fueled blizzard cannot deter genuine economic growth.

If President Trump sits down with his congressional partners and makes use of the lure of the "early repatriation window" to require minimum "famous investments" like Google's in other Rust Belt states, his industrial policy will have an enormous and visible impact. He doesn't have to say where specifically the new campuses need to go beyond the Great Lakes region (plus Iowa). He only needs to say that in order to grab the special repatriation rate, companies must have purchased land and telegraphed plans to employ at least one thousand people in each city they select by 2026. Presto. End of industrial policy. The Fourth Way nudges, it doesn't compel. The free market does the rest.

I know the objections of the *Wall Street Journal* Republicans. Screw 'em. The voters clearly rejected their NAFTA love. The deal-maker-in-chief gets it. That's why he got elected.

Here's the Fourth Way to harness his political capital to the greater good. (And by the way, the schools and infrastructure needed to support the spread of Silicon throughout the Great Lakes region already exist there. Unlike California, it also has plenty of water. And it has the kind of good government not dominated by organized labor, especially public employee unions. Go for it, President Trump. Make the Rust Belt shine and hum again.)

There remains this absurd tax code. I don't have a clue where to start beyond what not to do, but my pal Hank Adler does. Along the way—again in "retirement"—Hank's been a member of the board and audit committee chair for three real estate investment trusts with around $6–7 billion in assets, even as he worked ceaselessly to try to save Corinthian Colleges from their Obama administration–ordered demise. He's a former board member, treasurer, and audit committee chair for Hoag Hospital (one of California's health care jewels) and was the first chair of his city's—Irvine—Finance Commission, which created a financial plan that continues more than twenty years later to make Irvine financially viable. When he got bored he ran for and was elected to the Irvine Unified School District (IUSD) Board, where he served as president and helped create the plan that allowed IUSD to survive the Orange County bankruptcy. He has also been on the board of Orange County's New Directions for Women, which raised $1 million and purchased three homes for treatment of alcohol- and drug-dependent women. Hank's a great American. There are a thousand or even ten thousand Hanks, and by that I don't mean real smart, real experienced tax accountants who have lived in the code at very high hourly rates for decades. I mean experts who chose not to live in D.C. Nobody who lives in D.C. ever asks them for anything except money.

Hank has the deep smarts and real-world experience

to suggest what a tax reform—a real one—would look like. So go read Appendix D. It's about the simplicity. "KISS": Keep It Simple, Stupid.

I trust Hank. I love the career staffs on the Hill; some of my best friends are lobbyists. But I don't trust them. And I really don't trust the *Wall Street Journal* Republicans fresh from their Ludwig von Mises cruises on the Adriatic. The Fourth Way is reform bordered always with simplicity, and it ought to draw on real-world experts, not think-tank sharpies.

The whole Fourth Way will all be for naught if we don't tame and shrink the federal bureaucracy, and quickly.

Now I turn to those agencies, the vast archipelago of bureaucratic power centers that have grown up in D.C. over the past 75 years.

First, my credentials to write what I am about to write.

I ended my years in the Reagan Administration as Acting Director of the United States Office of Personnel Management. I had previously been confirmed by the Senate as the Deputy Director of the 6,000-person-strong human resources department of the vast federal civilian bureaucracy, having served as the agency's general counsel before that, and as general counsel of a much smaller agency—the National Endowment for the Humanities—and as an Assistant Counsel in the White House under the legendary Fred

Fielding and his remarkable deputy, Richard Hauser. Before that I had carried (highly classified) briefcases for both General William French Smith and Edwin Meese. The Reagan folks didn't care how old you were. They cared about whether you could get certain jobs done without much fuss and no scandals. So I rose. Rapidly.

At the end of my tenure I also ended up on something called the Administrative Conference of the United States. From the website of ACUS:

> ACUS is among the smallest agencies of our federal government, but it has a very important mission: to promote improvements in the efficiency, adequacy, and fairness of the procedures by which federal agencies conduct regulatory programs, administer grants and benefits, and perform related governmental functions. We do this through a variety of activities that include scholarly research projects, development of recommendations directed primarily to agencies and Congress, and publications and seminars on best procedural practices.

Now that sounds pretty good in theory, right? In practice the ACUS is a law professor's junket, because agencies decide their own ways, their own rules, pushed and pulled on the margins by Congress, the president, and the federal courts along the way. The theory of the federal administrative state—the theory of the progressive movement as a whole, actually—was that expertise would win out, staff these new agencies, conquer all ills, vanquish all unenlightened foes. In fact, agencies became fiefdoms, special interests, and massive vehicles of self-interest for those employed there. It would take a long book that very few people would read to detail all that has gone wrong with this massive bureaucracy that now numbers around 2.7 million federal civilian employees (and about 1.5 million Americans in federal military service). I believe this massive civilian bureaucracy is a threat to liberty. It can't just sit there. It has to do something. And mostly what it does is enforce existing rules and make new ones. Rules that usually were not authorized by Congress. Rules that are impossible to fight. Rules that drive average Americans crazy when they run into them, no matter the occasion and no matter the agency.

Most of my experience comes from my time "inside" the beast at OPM and ACUS, and from the thirty years of private law practice noted above, which primarily involved dealing with three agencies in particular: the U.S. Environmental Protection Agency (EPA), the U.S. Army Corps of Engineers (USACE), and the U.S. Fish and Wildlife Service (USFWS).

When I left the federal government, I immediately turned around and became a lawyer representing large landowners before these three agencies and their state counterparts. I processed permits, I dueled with bureaucrats, I came up with solutions to regulatory deadlocks over endangered species and "waters of the United States." While I genuinely came to like and respect a third of the feds with whom I dealt, two-thirds fell in my esteem to the lowest level. They were either incompetent or so ideologically invested in a process that they were as far from fair as I am from being a Steelers fan. Or both. Often both. Maddeningly both. And as the best retired, far worse replaced them.

The incompetent I could work with over time, wearing them down. The ideological fanatics—well, that took trips to D.C. and lawsuits. The overwhelmed or the simply lazy I felt sorry for. It isn't rewarding work when there is no reward for your work except a citation.

The free market will not flourish in the country until these three agencies are dismantled from top to bottom. They control the land and the businesses that can use the land. They are populated in key places by no-growth extremists and the fair-minded are cowed and afraid to move. The Fourth Way will empower new appointees to fire large numbers of tenured civil servants and do so peremptorily. A handful will be wrongly dismissed, but most are living on paychecks they do not really earn, the costs of which are contributed by people who work too hard to be so poorly served. Worst of all, these bureaucrats have ignored their missions. Had genuine environmentalists been in charge of the Fish and Wildlife

Service for the past thirty years, there wouldn't be an unfunded or unfinished habitat management plan for endangered species in the United States. They don't know how to do it. They lack the skills. If President Trump attended one week of meetings at any of these three agencies, he'd resign in despair.

The Fourth Way requires a massive rewrite of the Civil Service Reform Act of 1978. Agency heads must be able to fire 5 percent of their workforce for any reason whatsoever every year. That simple authority will do the trick. Impose on the individual bureaucrats the actual, genuine prospect of unemployment in the morning and they will show up, sit up, listen, and get to work.

VI

"Impeachment's Just Another Word for Nothing Left to Lose"

On Friday, November 11, 2016—three days after President Trump defeated former secretary of state Hillary Clinton for president—*New York Times* columnist David Brooks wasn't holding back. He wrote, "Trump's bigotry, dishonesty and promise-breaking will have to be denounced.

"We can't go morally numb," the ordinarily reserved Brooks continued. "But he needs to be replaced with a program that addresses the problems that fueled his ascent." Replaced?

"Metaphorically?" we readers asked.

No, not metaphorically, we quickly learned. "After all, the guy will probably resign or be impeached within a year," declared Brooks. "The future is closer than you think."

I had also been thinking about impeachment on the Friday after the election, but I was thinking about the three- to- five-year range, after a disastrous first two years led to a wipeout of Republicans at the polls in November 2018 and the corrosive effect of hyper-loyalists in President Trump's administration began to surface. The problem is never loyalty. Loyalty among political supporters is a good and necessary thing. Blind loyalty, though, is dangerous. That is G. Gordon Liddy and Chuck Colson territory, and married to John Dean timidity and moral smallness, a recipe for a replay of the Nixon tragedy—not as farce, but as another crisis.

Democrats would never impeach one of their own. Never. Republicans already have. And if all goes wrong, whether very quickly, as Brooks suggests, or possibly in a longer arc, as I fear is at least somewhat possible, then impeachment will be back in the news, as it already has been twice in my lifetime. I'm only sixty, and have vivid memories of two such instances, and now have to confess the idea of the impeachment of President Trump is hardly a fantasy.

Impeachments are political trials. Here is the entirety of the Constitution's statement on that subject:

> Article II, Section 4: The President, Vice President and all civil Officers of the United States, shall be removed from Office on Impeachment for, and Conviction of, Treason, Bribery, or other high Crimes and Misdemeanors.
>
> Article I, Section 3: The Senate shall have the

> sole Power to try all Impeachments. When sitting for that Purpose, they shall be on Oath or Affirmation. When the President of the United States is tried, the Chief Justice shall preside: And no Person shall be convicted without the Concurrence of two thirds of the Members present.
>
> Judgment in Cases of Impeachments shall not extend further than to removal from Office, and disqualification to hold and enjoy any Office of honor, Trust, or Profit under the United States, but the Party convicted shall nevertheless be liable and subject to Indictment, Trial, Judgment, and Punishment, according to Law.

That's it. Everything else is speculation. We have three precedents for why and how presidents are impeached, and two for how they are tried. There is one undeniable conclusion: Impeachments are about politics. The politics of the times in which they occur. Nothing else definitive can be said, even though scores of books and thousands of columns have been written in whole or part on the subject.

James Madison, who more than any man devised the Constitution and secured its ratification, took notes during the deliberations on the framing of the document in the summer of 1787 in Philadelphia's Independence Hall. Madison's famous "Notes" record his own statement on the subject of presidential impeachment, made on Friday, July 20, 1787:

> Mr. Madison thought it indispensable that some provision should be made for defending the Community agst. the incapacity, negligence or perfidy of the chief Magistrate. The imitation of the period of his service, was not a sufficient security. He might lose his capacity after his appointment. He might pervert his administration into a scheme of peculation or oppression. He might betray his trust to foreign powers. The case of the Executive Magistracy was very distinguishable, from that of the Legislature or of any other public body, holding offices of limited duration. It could not be presumed that all or even a majority of the members of an Assembly would either lose their capacity for discharging, or be bribed to betray, their trust. Besides the restraints of their personal integrity & honor, the difficulty of acting in concert for purposes of corruption was a security to the public. And if one or a few members only should be seduced, the soundness of the remaining members, would maintain the integrity and fidelity of the body. In the case of the Executive Magistracy which was to be administered by a single man, loss of capacity or corruption was more within the compass of probable events, and either of them might be fatal to the Republic.

The man next most responsible for ratification was Alexander Hamilton. In Federalist 65, published on March 7, 1788, Hamilton wrote about the sorts of "high crimes and misdemeanors" that the Constitution anticipates might be referred to the United States Senate from the United States House of Representatives:

> A well-constituted court for the trial of impeachments is an object not more to be desired than difficult to be obtained in a government wholly elective. The subjects of its jurisdiction are those offenses which proceed from the misconduct of public men, or, in other words, from the abuse or violation of some public trust. They are of a nature which may with peculiar propriety be denominated POLITICAL, as they relate chiefly to injuries done immediately to the society itself. The prosecution of them, for this reason, will seldom fail to agitate the passions of the whole community, and to divide it into parties more or less friendly or inimical to the accused. In many cases it will connect itself with the pre-existing factions, and will enlist all their animosities, partialities, influence, and interest on one side or on the other; and in such cases there will always be the greatest danger that the decision will be regulated more by the comparative strength of parties, than by the real demonstrations of innocence or guilt." (Emphasis added)

Both Madison and Hamilton are on record stating the "why" of impeachment. The Constitution lays out the how. If necessary in the eyes of a majority of the House members, the members can impeach a president in a day. If necessary in the eyes of two-thirds of the senators present, a president can be removed from office the same day as the impeachment articles are voted. There is no magic here. No necessary timeline.

There would be, as Hamilton predicted, plenty of agitated passions around any impeachment process, much less a quick one. I include just the law and the ideas of the two men most responsible for the law. The rest is chasing after wind. If President Trump proves reckless, he will be impeached, tried, and removed. If President Trump is proven corrupt, he will be impeached, tried, and removed. If President Trump abuses power, he will be impeached, tried, and removed.

Republicans have done this in the past. They will do it again if the country and party need it done. And if the party needed it done, they would do it. And the likelihood of the latter being fully included within the compass of the former is 100 percent. To be a party man (or woman) on issues of impeachment is, for Republicans at least, to be a patriot. The GOP has been tested on that before and did not fail. The Democrats did not convict their impeached president. Draw your own conclusions. But President Trump, who has begun his time of authority so well—his proposed appointments, though not without some controversy, are generally superb—is not likely to casually tempt the impeachment gods. He knows the history here. He will self-regulate.

It is his closest political aides—his most loyal, longest-serving aides—who would cause the ground underneath him to crumble. "He stood on pinnacles that dissolved into precipice," Dr. Kissinger said of Richard Nixon at the late president's funeral. "He achieved greatly, and he suffered deeply." This eulogy is a warning to Trump, a caution that Gerry Ford, like Mike Pence, was a welcome midwestern alternative to too much drama and too much abuse of power. The people have their limits. As does the Congress.

Knowing this, I expect President Trump to somewhat ruthlessly eject from his administration those who open up the boss to attacks. With so many knives so openly brandished from before his inauguration, it would be political insanity to indulge the blindly loyal their small dramas and petty rivalries and score-settlings.

President Trump's first appointments were excellent. His follow-through on staffing has been excellent. If he takes even a few of the suggestions in these pages his administration's launch will be spectacular.

But there is risk. It is outlined above. I genuinely hope this was the unnecessary chapter, the caution absurd in retrospect. We shall see.

VII

Conclusion

Radio hosts develop taglines. At times in my broadcast career I've referred to myself as "The Voice of Reason in the West," "Johnny Radio" (ill-fated, that one, but I hope the young man recovers and returns), and "Not perfect, just the best."

That last descriptor applies to the unlikeliest of years for me and for the country. When 2016 began I was riding a fine media wave, having participated as a panelist in two GOP presidential debates and planning to serve as a panelist in two more even as I moved to the morning drive syndicated radio slot in the East, the "big bus" of radio as I called it, when Bill Bennett retired in April 2016. While I knew I had another two debates on tap as Salem Media's panelist on the CNN stages, I didn't anticipate joining NBC and MSNBC as an analyst, going from an occasional *Meet the Press* panelist to a regular, or writing this book. Or, for that matter, that the Cavaliers would win an amazing NBA title (coming back from a 3–1 deficit to the Warriors!) or that the Indians would drag their injury-depleted club to extra innings in the seventh game of the World Series (damned rain delay, joining "Red Right 88," the Drive, the Fumble, the Shot, and Jose Mesa in Cleveland sports' hall of infamy) or that the Ohio State University Buckeyes would win their first-ever overtime game against Michigan (and a double overtime at that!).

I never believed, for a second, in all of 2015 or for the first four months of 2016, that Donald Trump would be the GOP nominee in November 2016. I thought he would implode over his attacks on Judge Curiel—calling those attacks "stage-four cancer" that would "kill the party if not reversed," and arguing in the middle of those attacks that Trump was heading the GOP plane "into the mountain." Then he pulled out of that nosedive. I campaigned for him, broadcast approvingly from the Cleveland convention, hit the road for his election . . . until the *Access Hollywood* tape surfaced. Then I used Twitter to call on him to quit the race. When he didn't, I was certain he was doomed. I voted for him, and urged others to do so, but I was still certain he was doomed.

I didn't see his election victory coming, and though I was confident of the Republicans holding the majority in the House of Representatives, I wasn't sure that Speaker Ryan would be able to call upon Senate Majority Leader McConnell as a colleague, and certainly not in partnership with President Trump and Vice President Pence.

I am hardly alone. It was an unexpected year, the

most unexpected ever, and here we are at the start of 2017 with an amazing opportunity ahead of us. The Fourth Way beckons. Donald Trump and his allies have it in their power to begin America again, this time along renewed constitutional lines.

If TPRM embrace the Fourth Way, the possibility of an American renaissance is real and indeed close at hand, because these ideas aren't mine; they are the Framers' and Lincoln's, explained here with new phrases and modern terminology.

As I told Justice Breyer five years ago, the Founders "knew liberty." That's what this book is built upon: their shared love of liberty and the ways today's temporary guardians of that legacy—TPRM—could build on and unleash anew the amazing energy our system provides to advance human flourishing.

Remember the key metric: the ongoing, incremental expansion of liberty and literacy at home and in a growing number of stable regimes around the world. President Trump can lead through four years in which that metric expands dramatically. He can indeed win and win and win.

Or he could fail. Terribly. Cataclysmically. Though it is hard to imagine he could fail in a more thorough way than President Obama failed, President Trump could indeed be worse than the president best known for six words and two sentences: "leading from behind," "red line," "JVs," and "If you like the plan you have, you can keep it. If you like the doctor you have, you can keep your doctor, too." That's a massive amount of failure in a small number of words. But President Trump can surpass that.

Or it could be a glorious and surprising time to be an American. It could be a wonderful time to be alive. We could be citizens who witness and participate in a massive shift in priorities toward freedom and in the principles at the heart of the Declaration, in the Preamble of the Constitution, and in the spirit of Lincoln's Second Inaugural Address.

That's why I began this book with those three documents: so you can easily return to them now and review them. I urge you to join me in wishing the best for our new president and his Article II and Article III partners as well as for the leadership in the sovereign states and indeed for the well-being of every American.

"Give the new guy a chance," President George W. Bush admonished me and five other talk show hosts in the Oval Office on the last Wednesday of his presidency, in January 2009. I pass that along to every reader now, and pray you will take it to heart. The Fourth Way can work for everyone. Its successes can be measured. Let's all hope the total of achievements is high and rising come 2020.

APPENDIX A

The Homestead Act of 1862

Rec[?] 21 May

Public 64

HR 125

Thirty-seventh

Congress of the United States

At the Second Session

BEGUN AND HELD AT THE CITY OF WASHINGTON

In the District of Columbia

On Monday the [second] day of December one thousand eight-hundred and sixty-one

AN ACT to secure homesteads to actual, settlers on the public domain.

Be it Enacted by the Senate and House of Representatives of the United States of America in Congress assembled, That any person who is the head of a family, or who has arrived at the age of twenty-one years, and is a citizen of the United States, or who shall have filed his declaration of intention to become such, as required by the naturalization laws of the United States, and who has never borne arms against the United States Government or given aid and comfort to its enemies, shall, from and after the first January, eighteen hundred and sixty-three, be entitled to enter one quarter section or a less quantity of unappropriated public lands, upon which said person may have filed a preemption claim, or which may, at the time the application is made, be subject to preemption at one dollar and twenty-five cents, or less, per acre; or eighty acres or less of such unappropriated lands, at two dollars and fifty cents per acre, to be located in a body, in conformity to the legal subdivisions of the public lands, and after the same shall have been surveyed: Provided, That any person owning and residing on land may, under the provisions of this act, enter other land lying contiguous to his or her said land, which shall not, with the land so already owned and occupied, exceed in the aggregate one hundred and sixty acres.

SEC. 2. And be it further enacted, That the person applying for the benefit of this act shall, upon application to the register of the land office in which he or she is about to make such entry, make affidavit before the said register or receiver that he or she is the head of a family, or is twenty-one years or more of age, or shall have performed service in the army or navy of the United States, and that he has never borne arms against the Government of the United States or given aid and comfort to its enemies, and that such application is made for his or her exclusive use and benefit, and that said entry is made for the purpose of actual settlement and cultivation, and not either directly or indirectly for the use or benefit of any other person or persons whomsoever; and upon filing the said affidavit with the register or receiver, and on payment of ten dollars, he or she shall thereupon be permitted to enter the quantity of land specified: Provided, however, That no certificate shall be given or patent issued therefor until the expiration of five years from the date of such entry; and if, at the expiration of such time, or at any time within two years thereafter, the person making such entry; or, if he be dead, his widow; or in case of her death, his heirs or devisee; or in case of a widow making such entry, her heirs or devisee, in case of her death; shall prove by two credible witnesses that he, she, or they have resided upon or cultivated the same for the term of five years immediately succeeding the time of filing the affidavit aforesaid, and shall make affidavit that no part of said land has been alienated, and that he has borne rue allegiance to the Government of the United States; then, in such case, he, she, or they, if at that time a citizen of the United States, shall be entitled to a patent, as in other cases provided for by law: And provided, further, That in case of the death of both father and mother, leaving an Infant child, or children, under twenty-one years of age, the right and fee shall ensure to the benefit of said infant child or children; and the executor, administrator, or guardian may, at any time within two years after the death of the surviving parent, and in accordance with the laws of the State in which such children for the time being have their domicil, sell said land for the benefit of said infants, but for no other purpose; and the purchaser shall acquire the absolute title by the purchase, and be entitled to a patent from the United States, on payment of the office fees and sum of money herein specified.

SEC. 3. And be it further enacted, That the register of the land office shall note all such applications on the tract books and plats of his office, and keep a register of all such entries, and make return thereof to the General Land Office, together with the proof upon which they have been founded.

SEC. 4. And be it further enacted, That no lands acquired under the provisions of this act shall in any event become liable to the satisfaction of any debt or debts contracted prior to the issuing of the patent therefor.

SEC. 5. And be it further enacted, That if, at any time after the filing of the affidavit, as required in the second section of this act, and before the expiration of the five years aforesaid, it shall be proven, after due notice to the settler, to the satisfaction of the register of the land office, that the person having filed such affidavit shall have actually changed his or her residence, or abandoned the said land for more than six months at any time, then and in that event the land so entered shall revert to the government.

SEC. 6. And be it further enacted, That no individual shall be permitted to acquire title to more than one quarter section under the provisions of this act; and that the Commissioner of the General Land Office is hereby required to prepare and issue such rules and regulations, consistent with this act, as shall be necessary and proper to carry its provisions into effect; and that the registers and receivers of the several land offices shall be entitled to receive the same compensation for any lands entered under the provisions of this act that they are now entitled to receive when the same quantity of land is entered with money, one half to be paid by the person making the application at the time of so doing, and the other half on the issue of the certificate by the person to whom it may be issued; but this shall not be construed to enlarge the maximum of compensation now prescribed by law for any register or receiver: Provided, That nothing contained in this act shall be so construed as to impair or interfere in any manner whatever with existing preemption rights: And provided, further, That all persons who may have filed their applications for a preemption right prior to the passage of this act, shall be entitled to all privileges of this act: Provided, further, That no person who has served, or may hereafter serve, for a period of not less than fourteen days in the army or navy of the United States, either regular or volunteer, under the laws thereof, during the existence of an actual war, domestic or foreign, shall be deprived of the benefits of this act on account of not having attained the age of twenty-one years.

SEC. 7. And be it further enacted, That the fifth section of the act entitled "An act in addition to an act more effectually to provide for the punishment of certain crimes against the United States, and for other purposes," approved the third of March, in the year eighteen hundred and fifty seven, shall extend to all oaths, affirmations, and affidavits, required or authorized by this act.

SEC. 8. And be it further enacted, That nothing in this act shall be so construed as to prevent any person who has availed him or herself of the benefits of the first section of this act, from paying the minimum price, or the price to which the same may have graduated, for the quantity of land so entered at any time before the expiration of the five years, and obtaining a patent therefor from the government, as in other cases provided by law, on making proof of settlement and cultivation as provided by existing laws granting preemption rights.

Galusha A. Grow
Speaker of the House of Representatives

Solomon Foot
President of the Senate Pro Tempore

Abraham Lincoln
President of the United States

APPENDIX B

The Military Rebuild

Scenarios for the United States Navy and United States Marine Corps

I start with the specifics put forward by Captain Jerry Hendrix (USN, Ret.), who took to the *National Interest* the week after the election and laid out one view that I reproduce with permission:

> President Elect Donald Trump, correctly understanding the current strategic environment, is committed to building a 350 ship Navy. This will set aside thirty years of steady declines in the size of the Navy and put those who would make themselves the United States' enemy on notice that the "irreplaceable nation" has picked up the mantle of leadership that it so recently cast off in an attempt to become more "normal" and less "dangerous." However, while 350 ships may seem huge in comparison to the battle force of 272 ships we have today; it actually represents the bare minimum that is actually required to maintain presence in the 18 maritime re-

gions where the United States has critical national interests.

The last time the US Navy had 350 ships in its inventory was in early 1998, at which time it had 12 carriers, 30 cruisers, 53 destroyers, 40 frigates and 70 fast attack submarines. Five years later the Navy crashed through the 300 ship mark on its way to the 272 ships it has today, which includes 10 carriers, 22 cruisers, 62 destroyers, no frigates and 54 fast attack submarines. Much of this decline has been driven by the fact that individual ship costs have gone up owing to new advanced technologies while the Navy's ship construction spending account has remained flat, driving the number of ships that can be purchased downward.

In addition, the Department of Defense's budget was slashed by nearly $80 billion per year from its 2011 projections due to President Obama placing a higher priority on domestic spending and the impact of the 2011 Budget Control Act sequester provisions. Both of these factors were disastrous for the nation's defense and the fact that the Navy's leadership was able to keep as many new ships under contract as it did, despite pressures from the Secretary of Defense, was nothing less than heroic. The Navy's budget today should be around $190 billion per year according to the last threat-based budget proposed by then Secretary of Defense Robert Gates in 2011, but instead it struggles with a $155 billion budget imposed by the administration he left in disappointment.

These downward driving budgetary pressures, as well as the increasingly evident erosion of American prestige in the international arena, would clearly have continued under a Clinton administration that presented itself as an Obama third term. These factors led to discussions, including a recent strategic choices war-game, that proposed tradeoffs within the present Navy budget to help increase the Navy's ship count in an attempt to increase presence and slow the disintegration of the international system of free trade. These discussions, which I either willingly participated in or led, included proposals to cut the overall carrier force in an attempt to grow the overall Navy while staying within the current Obama administration sequestered budget limits. Fortunately, those discussions ended with the election of Donald J. Trump and the retention of Republican majorities in the House and the Senate. We now have a President and a Congress committed to a "peace through strength navy" that will once again allow the United States to maintain global security and stability on the seas.

The problems identified with aircraft carriers can be corrected within the Trump Navy plan. The issue of the carrier's costs as a proportion of the Navy's shipbuilding budget (one Ford class carrier is nearly the equivalent of an entire year's shipbuilding budget) can be addressed both by increasing the shipbuilding budget to the level it would be at had the government continuously adjusted it for inflation over the past fifteen years, and by returning to a schedule wherein carriers are produced every four years rather than every five, a decision that the Navy made to save money in the short term but only increased the net cost of the ships over the long run. Changing the production schedule will also have the additional benefit of getting the force back to 12 carriers in a shorter time, a move that is critical if we are to take pressures off the carrier force and reduce their deployments from the 9–12 months periods of recent years back to the six month deployments of the Cold War. Additionally, the Navy should also look at technical challenges with catapults and arresting gear within the Ford carrier program itself in order to drive out inefficiencies and drive down costs.

The second problem was that of defending the carrier in the new anti-access/area denial environments that the Navy increasingly found itself in around the world. A 272 ship Navy simply does not have enough cruisers and destroyers to surround and protect each of the carriers it deploys, but a 350 ship Navy can generate enough platforms to protect a twelve carrier strike force. However, the key vulnerability of our carriers to attack is driven not by the threat or even the ships that surround them, but rather it is a product of the present composition of the carrier's air wing, which forces these large capital vessels to operate ahistorically close to land. Changing the composition of the carrier's embarked air wing is the key improvement the Navy can make in the near term to guarantee the success of its carrier strike groups in the future.

The aircraft carrier is a platform, but its air wing is the weapon it employs. At the height of the Cold War, the U.S. Navy increased the size of the aircraft carrier to carry large aircraft capable of delivering nuclear weapons deep inside the Soviet Union, and thus was born the "Super Carrier," large enough to launch and recover 80,000-pound aircraft. The only reason we have super carriers today is to be able to carry aircraft that can fly long distances. During the 1950s the average unrefueled range of the carrier's air wing was 1,200 miles with some aircraft able to go 1,800 miles to deliver their weapons. By the late 1970s the unrefueled range number had shrank somewhat to 900 miles, but the carrier had developed a strong organic tanking capability that could extend the range of its aircraft in flight to meet strategic requirements.

However, the end of the Cold War led defense leaders to make a number of false assumptions regarding the future security environment. The deep strike mission was given to the Air Force as it was assumed that there was no need for service redundancy in this capability and an entire generation of long range aircraft retired from the carrier's deck. The submarine threat to the carrier was assessed as low, and carrier-based aircraft and helicopters associated with the anti-submarine warfare mission were decommissioned and sent to the aircraft boneyard near Tucson, Arizona. Lastly, and most disastrously, it was assumed that carriers in the future would operate in permissive waters, allowing them to launch their aircraft close to their enemy's shores. This assumption placed a greater emphasis on carrier sortie generation rates while decreasing the importance of range within the carrier's air wing. Today, the air wing's average unrefueled range is around 500 miles and its organic mission tanking capability is significantly degraded when compared to the past.

If the twelve carrier, 350 ship, Navy described by President Elect Trump is to be credible and mission effective, part of the new administration's plan must address the shortfalls in the carrier air wing. The first and easiest move should be to pull the nearly 90 S-3B Viking antisubmarine aircraft with 9,000 hours of life still on their wings out of the Davis-Monthan Air Force Base boneyard and get them refurbished and back into the carrier air wing along with some additional anti-submarine helicopters. With both Russia and China deploying more advanced and quieter submarines, we need to ensure that our carrier force is protected from this threat.

Second, extend the range of the F/A-18 Super Hornets that we already have by completing testing of the conformal fuel tanks that are currently under development and accelerate their introduction to the fleet. These tanks can extend the range of the present air wing without significantly adversely affecting the performance characteristics of the aircraft. A combination of a longer ranged Super Hornet and the new F-35C Lightning II aircraft, which already has good range, will help the carrier to stand off further from emerging threats.

Third, push to get the unmanned MQ-25 organic mission tanker into the fleet quickly, and ensure that it integrates stealth characteristics into its initial baseline design. A stealthy organic tanker is critical when considering that China's J-20 seems designed for the mission of targeting the Air Force's large fleet of "Big Wing" refueling tankers. If one or two of these high value tankers are taken out early in the fight, the ability of the United States' fleet of F-22s and F-35s to reach their targets will be significantly compromised. However, four to six stealthy MQ-25s launched from a carrier deck with enough fuel to double the range of two F-35Cs each can change the calculus in the anti-access/area denial environment instantly. Additionally, a baseline MQ-25 design that includes basic stealthy characteristics can easily evolve to become an unmanned strike platform itself as technology evolves to allow for this capability. An air wing that includes longer ranged Hornets, Lightning IIs and an unmanned aerial strike vehicle would return the super carrier to its historical efficiency and lethality, and would be the truest expression of the vision expressed by the President Elect.

A 350 ship Navy will not solve all of the nation's problems. Years of neglect and whimsical foreign policy pronouncements of false red lines and "leading from behind" will have to be overcome, but 350 ships will allow the nation to begin protecting its interests in the 18 maritime regions of the world on a consistent and credible basis. The Navy needn't look exactly like it did the last time it had 350 ships; we have far more destroyers today than we did in the 1990s for instance, and they are far more lethal than their predecessors, so perhaps we can have fewer cruisers than we had in the past. Frigates, smaller, cheaper and of a more lethal design than the current Littoral Combat Ship, something more analogous to those built by our European allies perhaps, should be bought in large numbers to provide increased naval presence patrols. Presence, the importance of being there, often with very basic, low-end ships that are backed up by the threat of high-end ships, is often enough to uphold American interests. Lastly, the nation needs more fast attack submarines and more guided missile submarines. Today we have just shy of 60 of these quiet, stealthy platforms, but this number will fall far into the 40s during the 2020s before beginning to rise again in the 2030s. In the end we will need more than 70 of these boats to protect our interests.

All of these recommendations assume that the industrial base is in a position to support a buildup in the Navy. Years of decline during the Clinton, Bush and Obama administrations have wreaked havoc on the shipbuilding sector. Companies have downsized, laid off, or retired skilled workers or merged with other companies to remain afloat in troubled times. Going from building two Virginia Class submarines per year to four would not be as simple as adding more money to the ship construction account. Welders certified to work on nuclear powered vessels take a year or more to train and certify, and the companies involved cannot cut corners for fear of damaging their reputations and stock prices. Nor can companies plan long term production ramp ups unless the Congress gets strongly behind President Elect Trump's vision and commits the nation to a long term, multi-year, block-buy naval building program that includes both ships and aircraft.

Twelve carriers, 350 ships, and a longer ranged carrier air wing should be the basis for the United States' grand strategy going forward. We are a maritime nation. We have always been a maritime nation since our founding, and now there is a commitment to make the investments needed to execute a new maritime based national security strategy. This will be a national effort from the start, an effort that will rebuild Blue Collar jobs throughout the nation in support of our national defense, and while there will surely be challenges to come; there is at least a vision and a number (350) and a beginning on January 20, 2017.

Hendrix is a disruptive naval strategist who has written on both carrier vulnerability in an era of absurd budget restraints and on how to move to restore what was lost given realistic budgets. He should be on any team going forward on the rebuild.

So too is “Officer X,” a professional's professional. I asked him for a layman's guide on how to move fast to redress the reverse momentum of the seas—how to get to 350 ships, and the right ones. He responded:

> One of the smarter requirements Congress recently levied on the Pentagon, in Section 231 of Title 10 of the U.S. Code, is forcing the Navy to submit not just an annual budget request but a 30 year long range shipbuilding plan every year. This has allowed Congress and the public to track how the Pentagon is or is not properly resourcing shipbuilding over time. In its July 2016 report to Congress, the Navy forecasts having 287 warships in 2017. This number is far too small to meet our nation's defense needs and multiple military officials have testified to Congress that a large number of requirements for Navy presence go unfilled every year. To the Navy's credit, it has recognized its shortfall in fleet size and has largely protected shipbuilding from the effects of sequestration. However, refraining from cutting budgets is not the same ensuring the Navy has the ships and other resources it needs.
>
> The Navy's currently articulated plan would result in a modest growth to a total of 313 ships in 2025 as a two term Trump administration would come to an end. To

understand what that fleet would look like, let me describe the types of ships that make up the 313.

1. 11 Aircraft Carriers. These are the Navy's largest and most expensive warships, and they take the longest to build. They are nuclear powered and capable of operating nearly 100 fixed wing, high performance aircraft worldwide. They are the main platform by which the Navy projects power ashore and maintains large area sea control. New aircraft carriers are built by Huntington Ingalls Industries (HII) in Newport News, Virginia.

2. 100 Large Combatants. These are cruisers and destroyers. They provide defense against aircraft, cruise missile, and ballistic missiles to ships at sea and often forces ashore. They hunt submarines and fire land attack cruise missiles against shore based targets. They are the workhorses of the surface fleet. They are built in two locations: in Bath, Maine, by General Dynamics (GD) and HII in Pascagoula, Mississippi.

3. 32 Small Combatants. These are the ships of the controversial Littoral Combat Ship (LCS) class. Designed to defend against submarines, mines, and small surface craft, the class has been plagued with reliability problems and differing visions on how the ships are to be crewed and maintained. There is currently a program to increase these ships' lethality and the Navy has plans to start a study on its eventual replacement next year. There are two variants of LCS, one steel version built in

Marinette, Wisconsin, and an aluminum version built in Mobile, Alabama.

4. 47 Attack Submarines. These are the ships of the aging Los Angeles class, the Seawolf class, and the new Virginia class. They maintain sea control, conduct intelligence missions, and dominate the underwater domain. They are built in two locations: in Groton, Connecticut, by GD [General Dynamics] and HII in Newport News, Virginia.

5. 4 Cruise missile submarines. Submarines converted to carry large numbers of land attack cruise missiles to enable a rapid covert strike on enemy targets ashore. These are ships that began life as Ohio class ballistic missile submarine. They are no longer in construction and newer Virginia class attack submarines are being enlarged to carry out the missions of these ships when they retire.

6. 14 Ballistic missile submarines. The ships of the aging Ohio class. Provides the president a survivable nuclear deterrent. The replacements for these ships are planned to be built by GD in Groton, Connecticut.

7. 34 Amphibious Assault ships. These come in two sizes. The larger Aviation Assault ships carry 1,600 marines, their gear, and a large variety of both fixed-wing aircraft and helicopters. The small Dock Transport ships carry 800 marines, their gear, and a small number of helicopters. The rough ratio of ships is two small for every one large. These ships are built by HII in Pascagoula, Mississippi.

8. 30 Combat logistic ships. These ships carry fuel, food, spare parts, and ammunition to other surface ships. These ships are built mostly by GD in San Diego, California, but some smaller ships are built in other yards around the country.

9. 37 Support vessels. Ships used to move troop and equipment between theaters of operation, ships that support long-range ocean surveillance and research, some patrol craft for local operations, hospital ships, and ships used to preposition equipment around the world. These ships are built in a variety of yards around the country but the largest support vessels are built by GD in San Diego, California.

The Navy needs more of almost every type of ship in its inventory, but its most critical shortages are in attack submarines, large surface combatants, and aircraft carriers. According to the Navy's current plans, the shipbuilding budget will spend average $16.2 billion over the next five years. That will grow to roughly $19 billion per year from 2022 onward, to maintain the current plan and to begin to replace Ohio class submarines as they reach the end of their service life. The current plan builds an aircraft carrier every five years, 2 large surface combatants each year, 1–2 small surface combatants per year, 2 attack submarines per year, 3 ballistic missile submarines in the next 10 years (with 9 in the 10 years after that), 6 amphibious ships in the next 8 years, and roughly 1 combat logistics force and 1 support vessel per year for the next 8 years. That is what $16–$19 billion buys the Navy. Many analysts say these numbers are optimistic, so it will be imperative that the next administration's appointees responsible for the Navy's acquisition are experienced professionals.

What would a robust shipbuilding plan look like and what would it cost? To start, the most important thing the next administration can do is increase the number of combat-effective Navy ships as quickly as possible. There is sufficient current industrial capacity to add a large surface combatant and an attack submarine each year to the plan. This would not be cheap, adding about $4.5 billion to the yearly shipbuilding budget. However, over the next eight years, that would add 16 top quality surface ships and submarines to the force, either delivered or in construction. Additional capacity exists for 3 amphib and 6 small surface combatants to be added to the next eight years. The small surface combatants should either be the enhanced LCS or the eventual replacement if it is ready to start construction. The total cost for these 9 ships would run roughly $10 billion, but averaged out over 8 years they would add $1.25 billion per year. That would add a total of 25 ships to the current Navy plan at a cost of about an extra $6 billion a year, or a total shipbuilding budget of $25 billion per year.

Those 25 ships would yield a Navy of 338 by the end of an eight-year Trump presidency. There are still 12 more to both achieve the promised 350 and add an important component to the Navy's combat capability. Given the challenges of the South China Sea, Eastern Mediterranean, Persian Gulf, and other global hot spots, the Navy needs a small, lethal, fast, short-patrol-duration warship for presence and to threaten an adversary's vital shipping. The Navy has no such ships; however, Halter Marine in Moss Point, Mississippi, recently built four Ambassador Mk III class fast missile patrol boats for Egypt. These boats pack significant punch and could be deployed to hot spots around the world in groups of 4–6. Since they have already been built recently and the U.S. Navy owns the design, they could be put into production quickly at several shipyards around the country, including Bollinger in Louisiana, Aker in Philadelphia, and Vigor in Oregon, as well as the original builder, Halter in Mississippi. These 12 ships could be built for $4 billion over the next 8 years.

There are two final actions that the next administration should take that would not add to the immediate ship count but would add to the Navy's long-term health. First, building an aircraft carrier every 5 years is not enough. If production were accelerated to a carrier every three years the Navy would eventually get to the 15 carriers it really needs. However, a modern carrier takes seven to eight years to build, so spending the additional $1.5 billion a year on aircraft carriers is an exercise in good stewardship. Second, the Navy must maintain the current funding programmed to replace the Ohio class submarine.

So a robust shipbuilding program over the next eight years would need an additional $8 billion per year, roughly $24–28 billion per year total, and would result by 2025 in 350 ships either in service or in construction and nearing service, providing sufficient capacity to meet our maritime defense needs around the world.

So you see, the pros know how to get this done. It isn't "pie in the sky." And Robert O'Brien added a kicker for message: "If you want to be provocative, call for refurbishing the USS *Wisconsin* and *Iowa*. Both are still on the Navy's list. You could put a lot of VLS cells on them for missiles. It would be as much of a political statement as a naval one. Both ships are actually in really good shape. The Marines will love it."

So would most Americans who understand the Navy is America's ambassador to the world, showing the flag of freedom and defending our interests and the sealanes but also arriving wherever havoc has created distress. There is one long hallway in the Pentagon devoted to displays about the massive humanitarian missions for rescue and relief that the United States sends—led usually by a carrier group with its power and water production capabilities—whenever nature strikes a nation, friend or foe.

That's why President Trump called for the revitalized United States Navy. That's why the coordinate branches, guided by the amazing professionals at the Pentagon, need to respond with the "Navy Act of 2017" and do so quickly.

Understand there are pressing needs in the other branches and I am not excluding them, nor do I intend to put them in a lower priority. This discussion is only to emphasize that the start must come with the Navy. And quickly. And because we are first and foremost a sea power in this age of globalization, we also need to refurbish the Marines and fast.

For specifics on the USMC I turned to Major General Mel Spiese (USMC, Ret.), a very good friend who was kind enough to welcome me to Camp Pendleton when he was deputy commander of I Marine Expeditionary Force. We spent the day traveling about the base, talking to young Marines (I recall especially two young officers who flew helicopters, just back from Afghanistan who appeared not to need to shave but who explained the uses of their lethal machinery in terms even a journalist could understand, and one old gunny who seemed reluctant to let a civilian much less a journalist near any of the mounted rocket arrays). I've spent many hours with Mel and his wife, Filomena, talking about the Marines and what they need. Then I imposed on him for a written summary. Here it is:

> I made the comment that there was a time America had a Marine Corps because it chose to have one—that came from LtGen Brute Krulak's "(No) Bended Knee" speech under testimony for the Senate. America now has a Marine Corps because it must. Our threats are varied, from mobile non-state actors recognizing no borders, to growing peer and conventional threats that confront us broadly. We can see missions run the spectrum, from just needing near presence to send a message, to actual intervention, and that across that spectrum, from humanitarian assistance to peacekeeping and enforcement, as well as actual combat.
>
> We need to be able to secure areas vital to our national security—sea lane choke points as an example, either before or after they present a threat. We now operate from secure locations, primarily in the U.S., into locations that may be austere and opposed, meaning we not only need to bring with us what we need to fight and sustain ourselves, we may have to do it from a starting point of zero. And these responses do not just preclude the luxury of secure offload and assembly; they will come with little warning, requiring the movement of forces and even initial engagements before we have formed a complete plan of action, or can muster the heavy force necessary for ultimate resolution, from

Pusan to Afghanistan, from Lebanon to Somalia, and major combat operations twice in Iraq. Our national command authority needs flexibility in their options, hence flexibility in military actions and response.

This is about U.S. national interests and national security, first and foremost, not service parochialism.

Here is a list of actions—some nuanced, but all impactful. I will address shipping, aviation and overall readiness. I am not specifying requirements by ship numbers, rather operational requirements that should then determine adequate numbers. It is no less than the ever hopeful 33 amphibious ships—that number should look more like 37, and operational requirements can better drive that than war plans we tend to ignore.

The list speaks to shipping, aircraft production, and readiness, and manning of the Marine Corps and operational Marine Air Ground Task Forces.

1. Designate all amphibious ship as combatants, not auxiliaries. They need to be maintained and manned as major combatants, not auxiliaries.

2. Assess all forward deployed combat power inclusive of amphibious ships with embarked Marines beyond just the location of the forward deployed forces—the Navy overlooks and does not account for afloat Marine forces in combat power assessments, only the CVBGs.

3. Prescribe all future amphibious ships must be built with well decks. This could be legislative in nature.

4. Maintain 2 forward deployed, certified Amphibious Ready Group–Marine Expeditionary Units at all time, allowing greater flexibility for Combatant Commanders and the National Command Authority to influence and respond to crisis. This needs to drive both shipbuilding and readiness. The requirement for certified forces is to ensure ship availability allows for adequate training for crisis response forces, and not "eat" predeployment operational training to push ships out (a lesson from Beirut).

5. Maintain a 15 day surge capability for an amphibious Marine Expeditionary Brigade, and that can only include the compositing of 1 forward deployed ARG; at least 1 ARG-MEU must be maintained as a national strategic reserve in the event of a MEB operational deployment.

6. Maintain 2 afloat MEB-size Maritime Prepositioning Squadrons.

7. Prescribe only "gray" hull combatants compose the assault echelon of an amphibious MEB, limiting "black" hull commercial ships only for follow-on sustainment.

8. Prioritize and accelerate the development of new ship-to-shore connectors, inclusive of the replacement Assault Amphibious Vehicle, Air Cushioned Landing Craft, and Utility Landing Craft.

9. Require the Marine Corps to maintain at all times a trained crisis response capability of a MEB, exclusive of forward deployed crisis response forces. The MEB can be sourced worldwide. That requires the infusion of operations and maintenance funds for readiness, as well as flexibility in end strength management.

10. Accelerate and prioritize the fielding of F-35B to the Marine Corps. The Marines have participated in all air combat operations, from the Balkans to a decade and a half in the Mideast, and have held on to legacy strike platforms, forgoing F-22 and F/A-18E/F in order to lead the transition of both AV-8B and F/A-18A/C/D to F-35B.

11. Accelerate the development and fielding of CH-53K. Marine heavy lift, already outdated, has been overflown in the decade and a half of combat.

12. Infuse Marine aviation with funds to repair readiness, both aircraft availability and pilot proficiency. Marine aviation does not have the luxury of tiered readiness; deployment and combat plan requirements task Marine aviation relatively greater than the other services, and it is showing in the condition of the aircraft, and the residual impact on pilot proficiency.

13. Preserve current Marine Corps structure and allow flexibility in end strength, enabling the Commandant to review and consider the organization of the Marine infantry battalion and its included units, as well as newly required combat enablers, without considering the harvesting of structure with the organization review.

I am trying to be objective, not parochial, focusing

on national security and providing the National Command Authority the greatest latitude in decision making and responses around the globe.

The U.S. Marine Corps is poorly understood within our national security establishment, including DoD. It is generally considered a light infantry force, kind of like commandos, who can operate from the sea, with an associated image that is a bit of an anachronism in the modern world.

That runs counter to the reality of genuine tactical and operational creativity and innovation, operational and strategic flexibility, and unmatched success in combat operations. In some ways, reflective of its uniquely developed systems, represented by armored vehicles that come ashore from out at sea, to VSTOL 5th generation stealth strike aircraft, and tiltrotor assault support aircraft. In other ways, it is reflective of its organization unique in all the world, defying every military norm in existence.

No one integrates within tactical formations the combat power resident in the Marine inventory. The Marine Air Ground Task Force, regardless of deployment or employment construct, cannot be matched in flexibility, adaptability, and combat power at the tactical level providing operational and strategic flexibility. At the squadron level—lieutenant colonel—strike aircraft are mixed with rotary wing attack aircraft and heavy lift aircraft, with tiltrotor assault support, operating from an 844-foot airfield, at sea, at night, and in foul weather. Being pushed out the bottom of that airfield is ground combat power, inclusive of main battle tanks, large-caliber towed artillery, and light armored vehicles. All of that operating under the command of a colonel, independent and moving throughout the globe freely as required by the NCA.

Marine innovation and creativity go beyond just equipment and organization, but the integration of air-power with tactical ground formations, the tactical employment of helicopters, the concepts of prepositioned afloat equipment to vastly increase strategic mobility of combat power came from U.S. Marines, in addition to mastering operations from the sea, and keeping it viable even in our current world.

Some examples of the practical impact of the U.S. Marine Corps:

The establishment of the Norway Air Landed MEB was prepositioning a Marine Expeditionary Brigade equivalent of combat equipment in caves, to circumvent the competition for strategic lift in response to Soviet attacks into NATO. The Marines developed deployable arresting gear to operate F/A-18 strike aircraft from roads, recognizing the ability to get ramp space at airfields would be limited, and likely at risk.

MPF meant that the Marines had the first credible combat power ashore and deployed along the Saudi border with Kuwait in the First Gulf War—not just headquarters in the field to put a "flag" on the map. It is important to not forget that the "fixing action" by I MEF along the Gulf Coast in Kuwait achieved success and the breakthrough into Kuwait City, while the "Hail Mary" left flank attack of 3d Army was under way. I MEF made it to Baghdad to tear down the statue in OIF. This is no small task, and hardly the outcome of a small commando force, but major combat power in support of operations that speak to existential threats to the country.

The Marine Corps prepositioning program includes the ability to build out of nothing a tactical airfield, inclusive of arresting gear, and reconfigured ships that can carry an entire fixed-wing and rotary-wing Marine Aircraft Group with operational sustainment at sea.

The first conventional combat forces in Afghanistan were Marines. 2 Marine Expeditionary Units forward deployed were configured under a command element from a MEB deployed to Egypt for Exercise Bright Star, into Task Force 58, projecting combat power from the Indian Ocean into southern Afghanistan. The task was given to Marines not because of forward deployed combat power, rather its forward deployed combat support. The Army could not get to Afghanistan without C-17s, and C-17s could not operate until an airfield was opened. The choice of Marines was the ability to reconfigure on the fly, and the presence of the wide array of forward deployed capabilities allowed for a task of airfield opening to lead, with combat operations disrupting the enemy as inclusive to the primary airfield opening mission.

During Operation Anaconda, Army forces were facing greater resistance than anticipated and required otherwise absent combat support—light forces. Rotary-wing attack and heavy lift forward deployed with a MEU operating off the coast of Africa were moved nearly 1,000 NM, principally self-deployed, and in something like 92 hours from receipt of the warning order were answering calls for fire in the mountains of eastern Afghanistan (recall the Apache battalion trying to get to and operate in the Balkans).

On the day the MV Magellan Star was recovered by the Maritime Raid Force from a forward deployed MEU, that same MEU had strike aircraft over Afghanistan conducting Close Air Support, heavy life helicopters and KC-130s in Pakistan conducting humanitarian relief, and forces in Jordan conducting bilateral training, all operating independently under the command of the MEU and Amphibious Ready Group spanning some 5,000 miles.

The United States Marine Corps, operationally organized around its unique and unmatched air-ground task force, inclusive of strike aviation, operating at sea, offers the president his greatest and most flexible military response, regardless of crisis, short of nuclear war. Maintaining the Marine Corps as we understand it is a national security necessity and priority. If you think through Marine operations in the last 40 years and consider how the U.S. might respond absent those forces and those options, the outcomes would likely have been different.

APPENDIX C

President Trump's List of Twenty-One Potential Supreme Court Nominees

1. Keith Blackwell—age 42

Keith R. Blackwell is an associate justice of the Supreme Court of Georgia. He was appointed to this position by Governor Nathan Deal on June 25, 2012. Before that, he served as a judge on the Court of Appeals of Georgia. Keith Blackwell graduated from the University of Georgia before earning his J.D. from the University of Georgia School of Law. Blackwell served as a law clerk for judge J. L. Edmondson of the United States Court of Appeals for the Eleventh Circuit.

2. Charles Canady—age 62

Charles Terrance Canady is a justice of the Supreme Court of Florida, having previously served as chief justice from July 1, 2010, until June 30, 2012. Canady has been a Justice on the court since taking his seat in 2008. Canady graduated with a B.A. from Haverford College in 1976 and a J.D. from Yale Law School in 1979.

3. Steven Colloton—age 54

Steven Michael Colloton is a federal judge who has served on the United States Court of Appeals for the Eighth Circuit since being appointed by George W. Bush in 2003. Colloton earned his A.B. from Princeton University in 1985 and his law degree from Yale Law School in 1988. He clerked for Judge Laurence H. Silberman of the United States Court of Appeals for the D.C. Circuit from 1988 to 1989. He was then a law clerk for U.S. Chief Justice William H. Rehnquist from 1989 to 1990.

4. Allison Eid—age 51

Allison Hartwell Eid is the ninety-fifth justice of the Colorado Supreme Court, having been appointed to the post in 2006 by Republican governor Bill Owens. Eid earned her bachelor's degree from Stanford University before earning her J.D. at the University of Chicago Law School. After graduating from law school, Eid served as a law clerk for U.S. Fifth Circuit Court of Appeals Judge Jerry Edwin Smith and then for U.S. Supreme Court Justice Clarence Thomas.

5. Neil Gorsuch—age 49

Neil McGill Gorsuch is a federal judge on the United States Court of Appeals for the Tenth Circuit appointed by George W. Bush in 2006. He earned his J.D. from Harvard Law School and doctorate of legal philosophy from Oxford University. Gorsuch clerked for Judge David B. Sentelle on the United States Court of Appeals for the D.C. Circuit, and then for United States Supreme Court Justices Byron White and Anthony Kennedy.

6. Raymond Gruender—age 53

Raymond W. Gruender is a federal judge on the United States Court of Appeals for the Eighth Circuit appointed by George W. Bush in 2004. He attended Washington University in St. Louis and earned three degrees: an A.B., a J.D., and an MBA. In 2001 he became the United States attorney for the Eastern District of Missouri, a position he remained in until his confirmation to the Eighth Circuit.

7. Thomas Hardiman—age 51

Thomas Michael Hardiman is a federal judge on the United States Court of Appeals for the Third Circuit nominated by George W. Bush in 2006. He went to college at the University of Notre Dame, where he received a B.A. in 1987. He studied law at Georgetown University Law Center and received a J.D. in 1990.

8. Raymond Kethledge—age 50

Raymond M. Kethledge is a federal judge on the United States Court of Appeals for the Sixth Circuit appointed by George W. Bush in 2008. He graduated from the University of Michigan with a B.A. in 1989. He began law school at Wayne State University in 1990, but graduated magna cum laude from the University of Michigan Law School in 1993. Kethledge then clerked for Sixth Circuit Judge Ralph B. Guy Jr. in 1994. After finishing his clerkship, he became judiciary counsel to Michigan senator Spencer Abraham from 1995 to 1997. Following that, Kethledge clerked for United States Supreme Court Justice Anthony Kennedy in 1997.

9. Joan Larsen—age 48

Joan Larsen was appointed to the Michigan Supreme Court by Governor Rick Snyder on September 30, 2015. Larsen is a graduate of the Northwestern University School of Law, where she graduated first in her class. She clerked for David B. Sentelle of the U.S. Court of Appeals for the D.C. Circuit and for Justice Antonin Scalia of the U.S. Supreme Court.

10. Mike Lee—age 45

Michael Shumway Lee is an American politician and lawyer who has served in the U.S. Senate since January 3, 2011. Born in Mesa, Arizona, Lee is a graduate of Brigham Young University. Lee began his career as a clerk for the U.S. District Court for the District of Utah before serving as a clerk for future Supreme Court Justice Samuel Alito, who was then a judge on the Third Circuit Court.

11. Thomas Lee—age 52

Thomas Rex Lee is the associate chief justice on the Utah Supreme Court. His nomination by Gary Herbert unanimously passed a vote by the Utah Supreme Court Judiciary Committee and he was sworn in on July 19, 2010. He received his bachelor's in economics from Brigham Young University and his law degree from the University of Chicago Law School. After graduating from law school, he clerked for Justice Clarence Thomas of the Supreme Court of the United States and Judge J. Harvie Wilkinson III of the U.S. Court of Appeals for the Fourth Circuit.

12. Edward Mansfield—age 59

Edward Mansfield is a justice on the Iowa Supreme Court. He was appointed by Governor Terry Branstad and assumed office on February 23, 2011. Mansfield graduated from Harvard College in 1978 and Yale Law School in 1982. After law school Mansfield clerked for Judge Patrick Higginbotham of the United States Court of Appeals for the Fifth Circuit before entering private practice.

13. Federico Moreno—age 64

Federico Moreno is a district judge of the United States District Court for the Southern District of Florida. He was appointed by George H. W. Bush and assumed office on July 17, 1990. He graduated from the University of Notre Dame with a B.A. in 1974 and from the University of Miami School of Law with a J.D. in 1978. Moreno served as a judge on the Dade County Court from 1986 to 1987. He served as a judge on the Eleventh Judicial Circuit Court from 1987 to 1990.

14. William Pryor—age 54

William Holcombe "Bill" Pryor Jr. is a federal judge on the United States Court of Appeals for the Eleventh Circuit and a commissioner on the United States Sentencing Commission. He was appointed by George W. Bush and assumed office on February 20, 2004. He earned his B.A. from Northeast Louisiana University in 1984 (now University of Louisiana, Monroe) and his J.D. from Tulane University Law School in 1987. Pryor served as a law clerk to Judge John Minor Wisdom of the United States Court of Appeals for the Fifth Circuit from 1987 to 1988.

15. Margaret A. Ryan—age 52

Margaret A. "Meg" Ryan is a judge for the United States Court of Appeals for the Armed Forces. She joined the court in 2006 after being nominated by President George W. Bush. Ryan graduated from Knox College with a B.A. in 1985. Ryan then attended the University of Notre Dame Law School. Ryan was law clerk to Judge J. Michael Luttig on the United States Court of Appeals for the Fourth Circuit, and then to Justice Clarence Thomas on the United States Supreme Court in 2001–2002.

16. Amul Thapar—age 47

Amul Thapar is a United States federal judge on the United States District Court for the Eastern District of Kentucky. He was appointed by George W. Bush and assumed office on January 4, 2008. Thapar received a B.S. from Boston College in 1991 and a J.D. from Boalt Hall School of Law, University of California, Berkeley, in 1994. He was a law clerk to S. Arthur Spiegel of the United States District Court for the Southern District of Ohio from 1994 to 1996, and for Nathaniel R. Jones of the United States Court of Appeals for the Sixth Circuit from 1996 to 1997.

17. Timothy Tymkovich—age 60

Timothy Michael Tymkovich is the chief judge of the United States Court of Appeals for the Tenth Circuit. He was appointed by George W. Bush and assumed office on

April 1, 2003. Tymkovich received a B.A. from Colorado College in 1979 and his J.D. from the University of Colorado College of Law in 1982. He then clerked for Chief Justice William Erickson of the Colorado Supreme Court from 1982 to 1983.

18. David Stras—age 42

David Ryan Stras is an associate justice of the Minnesota Supreme Court. He was appointed by Governor Tim Pawlenty and assumed office on July 1, 2010. He received a B.A. and an MBA from the University of Kansas. In 1999 he earned a J.D. from the University of Kansas School of Law. Stras clerked on two federal courts of appeal, for Judges Melvin Brunetti on the United States Court of Appeals for the Ninth Circuit and J. Michael Luttig on the United States Court of Appeals for the Fourth Circuit.

19. Diane Sykes—age 59

Diane Schwerm Sykes is a federal judge on the United States Court of Appeals for the Seventh Circuit. She was appointed by George W. Bush and assumed office in 2004. She earned a B.S. degree in journalism at Northwestern University in 1980 and a J.D. at Marquette University Law School in 1984. After law school, Sykes clerked for Judge Terence T. Evans at the U.S. District Court for the Eastern District of Wisconsin.

20. Don Willett—age 50

Don R. Willett is a Justice on the Supreme Court of Texas. He was appointed by Governor Rick Perry on August 24,

2005. Willett received a triple-major BBA (economics, finance, public administration) from Baylor University in 1988. He received his J.D., along with an A.M. in political science, from Duke University in 1992. After law school, Willett clerked for Judge Jerre Stockton Williams at the United States Court of Appeals for the Fifth Circuit.

21. Robert Young—age 65

Robert P. Young Jr. is the Chief Justice of the Michigan Supreme Court. Young was first appointed to the Michigan Supreme Court in 1999, elected in 2000 and 2002, and again won reelection in 2010 for a term ending in 2019. He graduated from Harvard College in 1974 and from Harvard Law School in 1977. After private practice Young was appointed to the Michigan Court of Appeals, and later elevated to the Michigan Supreme Court.

APPENDIX D

Framing the Tax Reform Debate

Hank Adler

Tax Reform: Simplicity Plus a Reduction in Rates

In the context of what can be accomplished in the first ninety days of the Trump administration with respect to tax reform, there needs to be a reality check. Significant simplicity and some meaningful measure of expanding incentives for investment and savings can be achieved fairly easily. A small rate cut probably also can be achieved. That is quite a bit and trying to do too much more will be extremely difficult and if accomplished, the world of unintended consequences could have lasting impact.

Note that for individuals, there is a practical limit as to what can be done to further simplify itemized deductions without causing uneven benefit between residents of different states or dramatically harming our nonprofit institutions that hold together the social fabric of our nation.

Note that for both individuals and corporations who must calculate their income from operating businesses, simplicity in the calculation of taxable income cannot be accomplished without a disaster in terms of comparability, fairness, and a significant loss of federal revenue. With an income tax comes the complexity of ensuring that everyone plays by the same rules.

Individual Income Taxes: Simplicity

For individuals, simplicity should be defined as creating tax returns that most individuals can prepare without the help of a professional advisor or an expensive software package. Attempting to have a result where most Americans have a single-page tax return is not a realistic goal, but reducing the difficulty of calculating the tax is both a reasonable and accomplishable one. It is generally the mind-numbing varying calculations of federal tax that drive taxpayers to seek a tax professional or expensive software.

Thus the first step in individual tax reform is to require only a single calculation of the federal income tax. One, a single tax calculation: that is all that should be required. One should not need to be able to solve an algebraic calculation for three unknowns to prepare their annual federal income tax return. The number of tax rates is irrelevant. The taxpayer after calculating his or her taxable income should be able to go to a single chart and determine the tax.

To create a single tax calculation, tax reform must eliminate the alternative minimum tax, the net investment income tax, the additional Medicare tax, the Obamacare penalty tax, and the special capital gains tax rate. Tax reform can eliminate the capital gains tax rate while continuing to incent investment via a lower percentage of capital gain, dividend, and interest income being included in taxable income. Tax reform can also eliminate the three possible tax rates for varying types of capital gains.

Eliminating the capital gains tax rate and encouraging investment can be accomplished by applying a percentage to the amount of capital gains, dividends, and interest that would become part of taxable income. For example, if a taxpayer had $10,000 of capital gains, $300 of dividends, and $700 of interest, the three amounts could be added together and multiplied by a specific percentage. That amount would be included in taxable income. In this example, instead of a separate calculation, if the specific percentage for investment income was 50 percent, the taxpayer's return would include $5,500 in his or her taxable income. With this modest change, which was the manner in which capital gains appeared in the tax return decades ago, the Internal Revenue Code would continue to encourage investment and savings without the mind-numbing additional forms and calculations.

Simplicity demands that Social Security be untaxed up to a specific amount and the remainder fully taxed. If a taxpayer had $40,000 of Social Security income and the untaxed portion was $15,000, the taxpayer would include $25,000 in his or her tax return. This change would eliminate both a separate calculation, which is probably mostly ignored, determining how much Social Security income is considered taxable income, and the calculation of the appropriate percentage of that amount that is taxed.

Simplicity could eliminate the taxability of unemployment benefits while eliminating deductions for educator expenses and moving expenses. Put these ideas into the category of tax simplicity and fairness. Other special adjustments to gross income should be eliminated, but no one is going to be able to run the gauntlet of lobbyists and special interest groups to accomplish this in the first ninety days of the Trump administration.

Another reality is that itemized deductions have already been simplified dramatically over the past decades. Most of what are left could be referred to as "fan favorites." What are left are deductions that are either baked into the economic livelihood of the taxpayer or important to the social fabric of the greater community. (A blunderbuss approach of limiting itemized deductions to a specific amount would likely limit wealthy taxpayers to deducting only their taxes and provide no tax benefit to charitable contributions. Driving the local church or hospital out of business is an unlikely goal of tax reform.)

The medical deduction currently gives inconsistency new meaning. The taxpayer is "fined" if he or she has no medical insurance, but the taxpayer is allowed a medical deduction if medical expenses surpass 10 percent of his or her adjusted gross income. Assuming Obamacare disappears in its present form, the medical deduction as currently formulated likely needs little or no change.

The most difficult itemized deduction to consider is the state tax deduction. If one were truly starting from scratch, there would be no deduction for any taxes. End of discussion, it is a bad idea. But we are not starting from scratch. The difficulty today is the inconsistency of the impact of this deduction for citizens in different states and the reliance that taxpayers have placed on this deduction to plan their economic lives. The elimination of the tax deduction to California taxpayers would result in a significant tax increase, while in the South where state tax rates are considerably lower, taxpayers would see little impact in the removal of the tax deduction. If President Trump is going to represent every state and not see Republican candidates in high-tax-rate states crushed in 2018, tax reform is going to have to skip the removal of the state tax deduction. The potentiality of "tax reform" resulting in decreased federal income taxes in some states and increased federal income taxes in other states is bad politics if nothing else. A sad reality of accomplishing tax reform immediately is understanding the reality of the impact on the ground to current taxpayers.

If the American dream is to continue to include home ownership, we must maintain the home interest deduction. Interest rates will not remain low forever, and as interest rates rise, the home interest deduction becomes more and more important. The potential economic impacts of rising interest rates and a concomitant reduction of residential construction because of the loss of home interest deductibility could be catastrophic. Risking the economy is not a strong legislative priority as part of tax reform.

The most important itemized deduction is the itemized deduction taken annually by the smallest number of taxpayers. The casualty loss deduction must be retained. The taxpayer who loses everything in a significant earthquake, hurricane, or flood needs to be protected from paying federal income taxes. Imagine a taxpayer losing his or her family home in a Katrina-type event and not receiving any reduction in their federal income taxes. This is the most socially compelling of the itemized deductions.

Society hinges on and requires the deduction for charitable contributions. The benefit of charitable contributions to hospitals, universities, religious organizations, and the Red Cross along with thousands of other charities is far too great to risk an elimination of the charitable contribution deduction. If this deduction were eliminated, it is probable that many or most large donations from living taxpayers would decline or disappear. The ability to raise capital funds for our hospitals and churches would be seriously impaired. I have sat across the table from many wealthy taxpayers, and garnering that multimillion-dollar contributions for the local hospital is difficult enough without losing the tax deduction that accompanies the mega contribution.

That leaves miscellaneous deductions. The miscellaneous deduction should be eliminated. Any material employee expenses would need to be moved to the employer, where they already should reside. One lifetime curiosity of mine has been the ability to deduct the costs of tax planning, thereby giving a subsidy to taxpayers for planning to reduce their federal income taxes.

Tax reform should eliminate all calculations with respect to dependents and require the Internal Revenue Service to build the equivalent deductions into the tax tables.

The changes above, for 99 percent of individual taxpayers, would eliminate the need for a tax professional or an expensive software package to prepare their tax returns.

The concept of the refundable tax credits should also be reconsidered. I am swimming rapidly upstream with this recommendation. The Internal Revenue Code was initially designed to collect revenue, not dispense federal welfare. This would eliminate the highly popular Earned Income Credit to the extent it is refundable. If the federal government wishes to grant welfare to its citizens, it should do so through the welfare system, not the tax code. At a minimum, the Earned Income Credit should not be available for any dependent who is a resident in another country. A benefit of this small change would be the elimination of billions of dollars of tax fraud that results from the claiming of phantom dependents not resident in the United States.

Individual Income Taxes: Rates

Individual tax simplicity must be accompanied by lower tax rates. Simplicity without lowering tax rates would be contrary to the promises made in the 2016 presidential campaign. The magic here for the Treasury would be to dynamically score the impacts of simplicity and determine both the percentage of investment income not subject to tax and the ultimate tax rates necessary simultaneously.

The Estate Tax (Death Taxes)

Only about ten thousand tax returns are required annually for estate tax purposes. Many fewer than the ten thousand estate tax returns filed result in a federal estate tax. An individual's estate is not subject to estate taxes unless it exceeds $5 million, and a married couple is exempt unless their assets exceed $10 million. Hence the estate tax is limited to a very few taxpayers.

The estate tax presents very difficult issues; urban legend supports certain "facts" that are not facts. This makes the discussion about the propriety of an estate tax in general quite difficult. The major piece of miscommunication with respect to estate taxes is that all or most of the assets in the estate have already been taxed. Whether it be the result of an individual holding assets that have massively appreciated in value or the result of great tax planning (i.e., tax-free exchanges), very significant parts of wealthy individuals' assets have not been previously taxed at the time of death. Consider both Bill Gates, the founder of Microsoft, and Mark Zuckerberg, the founder of Facebook. Neither of these individuals has paid any federal income tax on their current ownership of Microsoft or Facebook stock. Each has experienced literally no tax on the major portion of the wealth that they have accumulated. President-elect Trump has also apparently not paid very much in federal income taxes on the $10 billion net worth he has accumulated.

President-elect Trump has proposed the elimination of the estate tax.

There exists an issue of fairness in the ability of an individual to create massive amounts of net worth during his or her life without paying federal taxes and then being able to pass that net worth to the next generation tax-free. "Bob," the average Joe, has paid a percentage of his income to the government for his entire life. "Bob" should not be the only one paying taxes to keep the army armed.

There is also the very significant political element to President Trump sponsoring a tax reform package to eliminate a tax that would result in the elimination of a $5 billion future tax bill for him personally and similar tax benefits for many members of his cabinet. Forgetting any intellectual discussion, a president of the United States signing a bill that would result in an increase in his family's net worth of $5 billion could be political suicide. Maybe it should be.

Churches, hospitals, and universities would be victims of an end to the estate tax. The unlimited deductibility of contributions to charity at death is a major feature of the estate tax calculation. This incentive for charitable giving results in literally billions of dollars of charitable contributions from estates to charitable institutions for major capital improvements. One need only walk through a hospital or on the campus of a private or public university to see the benefits of deductible charitable contributions through the estates of the individuals. Buildings are named after these philanthropic decedents. Many of these charitable enterprises serve tens of millions of Americans every day. Major capital contributions do not result from the weekly collection plate. Part of the long-term future of our charitable organizations is through the deductibility of contributions upon death. No one has identified the new source of such funds if the estate tax is eliminated.

Most of the solutions to the problem of income being taxed twice upon death require a knowledge of the cost of the assets owned by the decedent. These solutions usually embrace the idea of a capital gains tax at death or a carryover basis to the heirs. The accompanying problem with both proposals is that the decedent cannot answer questions about his or her books and records after his or her death. As a result, a tax on capital gains at death or carryover basis for heirs would result in countless issues in proving the vitality of tax filings upon death or ultimate sale of the assets. Imagine the taxpayer with no records of the purchase prices of Dad's $10 million collection of stamps or paintings. The Internal Revenue Service will have a single answer to the basis for calculating gain on sale: zero.

There are a few opportunities that could be accomplished with initial tax reform with respect to the estate tax. The $5 million threshold could be raised, rates could be lowered, and/or payments could be made over a few years rather than nine months after death. Any of these changes would be welcomed by the few families that pay estate taxes and would not have the deep aroma of the Trump administration lowering taxes for themselves and their pals. An elimination of the estate tax as a political issue could stalk the Trump administration no differently than Hillary's email issues stalked Hillary Clinton.

Business and Corporate Taxes

One anomaly of the current U.S. tax rate is that virtually the only companies in the world that pay the top rate of the U.S. tax are companies that only operate in the United States. International companies can effectively tax-plan around the U.S. tax. Note Google and the other large tech companies generally pay very little in U.S. taxes as a percentage of their earnings. This is a grotesque result and must change.

The notion that business taxes are too high is entirely accurate. The U.S. tax rate on business is far too high and helps make American products less competitive on world markets. This high tax rate has resulted in American companies moving overseas, being acquired by foreign entities, and creating tax strategies that are solely for the purpose of reducing taxes paid to the federal government. Rates need to be lower to keep U.S. companies along with both white-collar and blue-collar jobs in this country. Lower tax corporate rates are an essential tool to this result. The idea of a corporate rate of 15 percent is a good one.

Repatriating income trapped overseas is a tax reform

"must do." Returning as much as $2 trillion into the United States for future U.S. investment is more than a constructive idea, it is an imperative. If one believes as I do that free markets are the best determiner for the allocation of capital, an argument can be made for a very, very low tax rate on repatriation. To the extent taxes are collected, reducing the national debt is not the worst idea in the world. To the extent the funds are retained by the receiving corporations, the best decisions will be made by the free market on how to invest the funds, not any requirement of specific law.

The long-term issue is creating a tax system that does not drive profits or jobs overseas and thereby create an instant redo of building up another $2 billion of earnings trapped overseas because of U.S. tax law. The scenario of the $2 trillion trapped overseas being repatriated at a very low tax rate and then being reinvested overseas is unnerving.

In the international arena, the United States is probably best served by adopting a modified territorial system with earnings earned overseas generally not subject to U.S. taxes. The modifications would have to comply with all U.S. treaties and be carefully constructed. This issue is better served outside the ninety-day first-term Trump administration window but needs be addressed reasonably quickly. The lowering of the tax rate to 15 percent and the repatriation of funds trapped overseas would be a great first step.

Finally on business taxation, the notion of taxing business profits earned by individuals at the lower 15 percent rate is a poor idea. The complexity of determining which businesses should be taxed at 15 percent would be a nightmare. Having all the individual business owners taxed at 15 percent and their key employees taxed at the higher individual rates would be no more than a formula for a campaign issue in 2018 against Republican congressional candidates. If a business wants a 15 percent tax rate, it needs to decide to become a corporation.

Final Thoughts

Ninety days is not much time to accomplish great tax reform legislation. If the administration would focus on simplicity, rewards for capital investment, and a concomitant reduction in tax rates for both individuals and corporations along with a super-low repatriation tax rate, it may be able to appropriately raise the victory flag.

Acknowledgments

My thanks to Jonathan Karp and Priscilla Painton of Simon & Schuster for encouraging this book and enabling its publication in such rapid fashion, and to Bob Barnett, who, though deeply wounded by the loss his friend suffered and the discouragement of dear colleagues far and wide, is a professional's professional and guided what was to have been a book about the GOP amid the ruins into a book about how the GOP can remain atop a very unexpected summit.

My colleagues at Salem Media—Edward Atsinger, Stu Epperson, David Santrella, David Evans, Phil Boyce, Tom Tradup, David Spady, Russ Hauth, Russ Shubin, and two dozen more—trusted me to represent the company at the four presidential debates in which Salem partnered with CNN, and CNN's Jeff Zucker, Jake Tapper, Wolf Blitzer, and the amazing Dana Bash (who split wide right with me all four debates) and the *Washington Times*'s Stephen Dinan, who joined us at the Miami debate, as well as the vast team at CNN Debate HQ that floated from city to city—especially the uniquely gifted and verbally talented Mark Preston and the always-preparing Eric Sherling—gave me a ringside at history and prepared me to succeed. Thanks to them all.

Andy Lack recruited me to NBC and MSNBC, where Elena Nachmanoff, Liza Easton, and Amelia Acosta have made every day a joy and where everyone from Tom Brokaw to the newest intern has been as welcoming as anyone could hope. Special thanks to Brett Holey and Jeff Coneys for teaching the technically challenged how to cope.

Diana Loveless has managed the circus very well indeed—many, many thanks—and the home team—Duane Patterson, Adam Ramsey, Jake Browatzke, Ben Bryggman, Anthony Ochoa, Will and James Hewitt, and Rob Lockwood—have never stopped producing. A special thanks to Marlon Bateman, who even after he left the team continued to send help to HQ. Thanks to them all.

Thanks to General Mel Spiese, Ambassador Robert O'Brien, Captain Jerry Hendrix, Officer "X," and Hank Adler for the specific expertise used in this book and to my colleagues at Larson O'Brien LLP and the Fowler School of Law at Chapman University for indulging my long absences in 2015 and 2016.

I conducted 170 candidate interviews with would-be GOP nominees on the radio in 2015 and 2016, fifteen with the new president. Thanks to every candidate and their professional teams. The GOP has a deep bench. Those fifteen interviews I owe to the always professional and responsive Hope Hicks (and Rhona!) and the rest of the Trump Organization team. Even when we were in disagreement, the new president and his team kept it professional.

Three friends keep me grounded with regular streams of abusive taunts about sports mostly, but also my haircuts, neckwear, and watches. To Lobdell, Caitlin, and O'Connor: the Cavs won the greatest comeback in NBA history, the Indians were robbed by a rain delay, the Browns are on plan, and the Ohio State University Buckeyes remain, as is widely and objectively reported, the best sports program in the land.

To the men and women in uniform, present and past, special thanks for keeping us safe and free so that we can write such books. Kurt Schlicter is your muse, and to my active-duty friends especially, thank you.

I also want to thank my weekly radio guests: Senator Tom Cotton, Congressman and CIA director designate Mike Pompeo, Mike Allen, David Drucker, Jim Talent, and Sonny Bunch. To the legion of almost-weekly guests, thank you as well for your frequent appearances. Good radio—indeed all good media—depends on the willingness of guests to show up and chat. To my left-of-center semiregulars Jonathan Alter, David Axelrod, E. J. Dionne, and Nicholas Kristof, a special thanks.

And to Betsy, "the Fetching Mrs. Hewitt" as she is known on the air, endless thanks for endless patience, grace, and love.